COME FLY WITH ME

BY

Wayne Fox

Cover designed by Wayne Fox, Author: Wayne Fox
tailhookpilot@gmail.com

Printed in the United States of America

First Printing: December 2020

ISBN-9798572412253

DEDICATION

This book is dedicated to the men I flew with in the Navy. I have a special remembrance for those who lost their lives. There were so many.

A poem I wrote for my friends who gave their lives as Naval Aviators.

LAST FLIGHT

Through a long and sleepless night,
I think of you, my friend.
You have flown your last flight,
so now we reach the end.

Once you roamed where eagles fly,
in planes of power and grace.
Up into the heavens so high,
you could touch an angel's face.

You have traveled through the air
and seen the power of God.
In darkening storm or sunlight fair,
you have gone where few will trod.

I no longer speak your name,
for deep inside, I hide a fear.
You are with me just the same,
but could my end be also near?

No one can see the tears I hide,
for men are not allowed to cry.
You are always at my side,
until we once more share the sky
Foxy

Foreword

This book is a revision of the original 'A Time to Remember'. I have lengthened it to give a more complete story with more attention to major events that happened. The main events in this book are real and actually happened. The dialogue is as close as I could recall, but may not be exactly as it unfolded leading up to that event. The minor happenings described are the typical life of a fighter pilot and follow the flow of the life we lived. The end results are as accurate as I can recall. They perhaps took a slightly different path, but they arrived at the same destination. It portrays the seven-plus years I spent in the Navy in the 1950s. Most occurred over 65 years ago, and time has dimmed my memory for some of the details.

I have tried to be very accurate in the outcome. I used the actual names of the people I wrote about unless I felt it was prudent not to do so. There are very few of those times in this book. The men who lost their lives are real, and their names are their real names. The major events are actual and did happen. Some things are not possible to forget, even though you would prefer to do so.

In January 1951, I joined the Navy as an enlisted man. I was selected for pilot training after nine months of service. I completed flight training and received my wings and commission as an Ensign in April 1953. After completing All-Weather School and jet training, I joined my squadron, VF-91, in August 1953. During that time, I flew jet fighters,

F9F-6 Cougars, and was stationed at the Alameda Naval Air Station, or on the aircraft carrier USS Hornet CVA-12.

I later returned to the training command in March 1955 as a flight instructor. In April 1956, I left the Navy to attend college. I requested a recall to active duty in November 1957. I was assigned to the instructor's school as a staff instructor until I left the Navy in November 1959.

In my seven-plus years in the Navy, I logged over 2,000 hours of flight time and over 4,000 landings. I was in six accidents or mishaps.

My friend Sam Hubbard reached the rank of Rear Admiral. In his career, he had command of the aircraft carrier Kitty Hawk. He was also in charge of pilot training and manpower in the navy.

My friend Bill Russ was the commanding officer of an F8U Crusader reserve fighter squadron and retired at the rank of Captain.

My friend Mac McMurtry was also the commanding officer of a fighter squadron and retired with the rank of Captain.

My friend Tom Cassidy was a Rear Admiral and held many command positions.

Lt. Wayne Fox, when leaving the Navy in 1959.

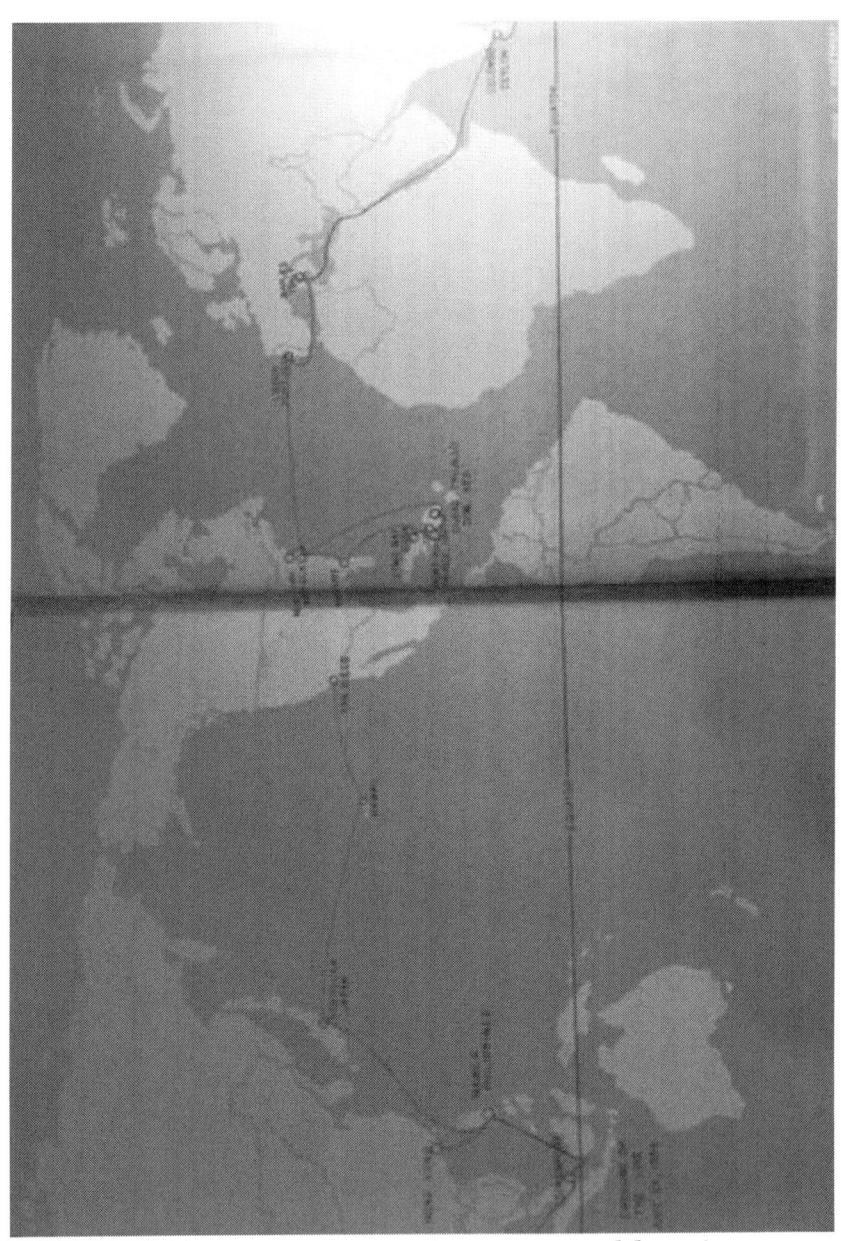

The route we followed on our world cruise

CONTENTS

CHAPTER I 11

CHAPTER II 23

CHAPTER III 39

CHAPTER IV 51

CHAPTER V 59

CHAPTER VI 69

CHAPTER VII 79

CHAPTER VIII 95

CHAPTER IX 111

CHAPTER X 119

CHAPTER XI 127

CHAPTER XII 141

CHAPTER XIII 163

CHAPTER XIV 173

CHAPTER I

AT SEA

I often spent leisure time in a gun tub just outside our bunk room. It was a place of escape, a place that seemed to be separated from the rest of the aircraft carrier and in a different world. It was a place that you could enjoy with your friends or just enjoy the solitude of being alone. I was there now, alone. My thoughts drifted to what we were doing and where I was in my life. I subconsciously took inventory of where I was and my present surroundings.

I was one of thirty-one pilots with twenty planes in fighter squadron VF-91 of Air Group 9 aboard the aircraft carrier USS Hornet CVA-12. Air Group 9 consisted of four squadrons, VF-91, 93, 94, and VA-95. VF-91 was the main fighter squadron, flying F9F-6 swept winged Cougars, whose primary purpose was to engage enemy aircraft in aerial combat. We could fulfill other roles such as ground strafing, but our primary purpose was to deal with enemy aircraft. We did not have rocket rails or bomb racks, so we lacked the capability of even carrying such ordinance necessary for ground or sea support.

Our planes were also equipped with a new radar-controlled gun site capable of calculating the lead that was necessary to hit a moving target. It could take into consideration such factors as increased gravity force that was often a factor in a gunnery run on a moving target.

The more exciting feature was that the Cougar was the Navy's first operational fighter that could break the sound barrier. The sound barrier is encountered at a speed of approximately seven hundred and fifty miles per hour.

We also had what was called a flying tail. We could lock the elevator in place, which controlled the pitch, or up and down control, moving the entire horizontal stabilizer as one unit. The horizontal stabilizer is the horizontal section of the tail. This increased our ability to make sharper turns. A sharper turn was a major factor in a dog fight. It gave you the ability to turn inside an enemy plane and bring your guns to bear when experiencing increased G forces. There was a major problem with the flying tail, which I will go into more detail about later.

VF-93 and 94 were attack squadrons and flew the F9F-5 Panther jet. The Panther was a straight wing subsonic aircraft designed for attacking ground or sea targets. They were composed of a smaller number of planes and pilots than VF-91.

The last squadron, VA-95, flew the AD Skyraider. This was a propeller-driven attack plane. It was a workhorse. It could carry a larger payload than any of the other planes on board the Hornet. VA-95 also had fewer planes and pilots than VF-91.

We also had a small contingency of photo planes and pilots. They were flying the F2H-3n Banshee jet. This airplane was designed for the job it did.

We were on a cruise in 1954, which was to last for nine months. The Angled Deck had not yet been designed, so we were operating off a straight deck. On a straight deck, if you failed to pick up an arresting wire with your tailhook on landing, you were destined for the crash barriers. These barriers were composed of several Davis barriers first. The Davis barriers were about three feet off the deck and were designed so that when the nose wheel contacted them, a lower wire was flipped up and engaged the main landing gear for a more positive stop. If the Davis barriers failed to stop the airplane, a twelve-foot high barrier called the Palisade was the last chance. It was composed of vertical nylon strapping that would grab the plane and hopefully stop it.

One major problem could be encountered if you hit the Palisade. As it collapsed around the airplane, the top wire could slide up the nose and jump into the cockpit, catching the pilot at the throat level. To prevent this, when the tailhook was extended, a hook came up in front of the windshield as well. This was designed to catch the top wire before it could get into the cockpit. However, it was possible that the hook may not catch the wire, therefore it was advisable to get your head down if you were going to engage the Palisade. This was not an easy thing to do since you had shoulder straps that held you firmly in place. I was not sure it was even possible to get my head down low enough for the top wire to pass over my head, but when I engaged this barrier on my only such landing, I had my head down so low I hit the gunsight with my helmet.

Carrier landings could be exciting. Landing on a pitching deck in high seas was extremely challenging. When we operated under these conditions, the LSO (Landing Signal Officer) stood on a platform at the end of the flight deck and guided the planes in with hand wands or paddles. He had a man beside him telling him if the deck was coming up or going down. The LSO had to signal the pilot to cut (A signal by bringing his right arm and paddle across his chest to tell the pilot to close the throttle) power to the engine and land the plane at exactly the right time so a wire would be engaged. If he cut a plane for landing when the deck was coming up, the plane could slam into the deck and cause a landing gear failure. It could also bounce over the barriers which happened once while we were on this cruise. If the plane was cut for landing when the deck was falling away, it was possible to miss all or most of the wires. In our jets, we came over the rear, or fantail, of the carrier at about 140 miles per hour. The speed of the carrier put us in the vicinity of 100 miles per hour when we made contact with the deck. The airplane would be stopped in about two or three hundred feet.

It was also necessary for the jets to be catapulted off the deck since they did not have enough deck run to gain enough speed to get into the air under their own power. The catapults were two hundred feet long. In this distance, you would accelerate about one hundred miles per hour in those two hundred feet and about two or three seconds. It was necessary to prepare yourself for this acceleration. When the

Catapult officer gave you the full power signal, which was a raised hand in a circling motion, you applied full power and prepared yourself for the sudden acceleration. A rod was pulled up in front of the throttle that was grasped along with the throttle, so the sudden acceleration did not make you pull the throttle back. Your other hand was placed behind the stick with your elbow in your stomach to avoid pulling the stick back. When you were ready, a salute was given to the launch officer telling him you were ready. Your head was then placed firmly against the headrest. When the Launch Officer dropped his upheld hand and pointed down the deck, the catapult is fired. It is impossible to make any movement in the sudden acceleration that follows.

It may be of interest to know that the only thing holding you in place before the shot is an aluminum band holding two overlapping steel rods together. When the catapult is fired, the aluminum band breaks and allows the rods to separate, thus freeing the plane. This was true back in the 1950s. I assume that may no longer be the method used.

As I was getting up to leave, the loudspeaker crackled a couple of times and announced that all pilots were to report to their ready room. It was for no particular reason; pilots were just told to report to their respective ready rooms. I was going there anyway, so it was not necessary to alter my course.

As I approached our ready room, pilots were taking their seats, so I joined them. Everyone was offering his opinion on why we were called there. The speculations were endless. As the Skipper entered the ready room, we were called to attention, which was only done when something important is in the air.

"Please be seated, gentlemen." His words came out loud and clear, which added authority to what he was about to announce. There was a rather long pause as his eyes swept the pilots. "Gentlemen, we have just received word that an airliner has been shot down near Hainan. They are not sure who is responsible, but there is little doubt who it is. We are quite certain it was a surface-to-air missile, but we are not sure just where it came from. It could have been mainland China or Hainan. We are going there with the premise of looking for survivors. It is very unlikely that anyone could have survived. Still, we need to show our strength and demonstrate our objection to such a hostile act."

"We may encounter Chinese Mig jet fighters or other prop fighters. However, it would be foolish on their part to challenge us, unless they are stronger than we think they are. Our entire battle group of all four carriers is now steaming toward Hainan. We will be close enough to launch aircraft tomorrow morning. We do not have the plan completed, but I feel we will launch the Skyraiders (Propeller driven dive-bombers) first, followed by Panthers (F9F-5 jet attack planes) with rockets. Our squadron will follow and fly cover at about 40,000 feet in case Migs show up."

"We will have the schedule out shortly, so you can prepare yourself. Are there any questions?" The Skipper hesitated for a short time with no questions being asked. All came to attention as he left the room.

I stopped to see if my flight had been canceled, but found it was still on the schedule. As I was looking at the schedule board, the duty officer arrived and told me my flight had just been canceled. "They want to keep all the planes ready for tomorrow if possible," he offered as an explanation. I offered my thanks for the information and walked down to the bunkroom I shared with the other junior pilots.

We had several cubicles in that area with four bunks in each cubicle. I had one of the lower bunks in the first cubicle. Across from me in the lower bunk was my close friend Sam Hubbard. Above my bunk was Jim Hargrove, and across from him was Lee Pritcher. We were all Ensigns, very new to flying. Sam and I had known each other in the training command, but we had not lived together until we were assigned to VF-91.

My name is Wayne Fox, and I go by the nickname Foxy. We had the before mentioned gun tub that sported twin three-inch guns just outside our room on the catwalk. It was our private lounge and sanctuary. Many hot nights were spent there, or on the flight deck when it was too unbearable to sleep in our bunk room. I headed for our private sanctuary, which also seemed to be our safe place. All worries and cares could be cast into the ocean from there. Sam was already there when I arrived. He was at ease and very relaxed. We were two friends who just wanted to pass the time of day. "What do you think is going down?" I asked.

Sam replied, "I'm not sure what to expect, but with four aircraft carriers, we are going to flex a lot of muscle. If they try to engage us, they better have a lot of that muscle themselves. I think they'll lie low and let us do our thing."

"I think you're right on that, Sam, but sometimes people do stupid things. I think a lot of it depends on how much muscle they have in the area, or how fast they can bring in more. We'll just have to wait and see. We have about 300 planes with four carriers. There's also a cruiser and several destroyers with us. I cannot think they would want to mess with us unless they have something we don't know about."

Sam hesitated and then offered, "I think I'll write a letter to my parents before we go check to see if we will be flying in the morning. Let me know when you're ready to go to the ready room."

"Will do, I think I'll get a letter off as well. My sister had many questions in her last letter that I should answer. See you later." With that, we both left the gun tub. Sam stopped at one of the desks we had in a separate area, but I decided to lie down for a couple of minutes.

It will be difficult not to think about tomorrow and guess what might take place. It could be a walk in the park or a look at hell. I had never seen combat, and that was also the case for all the other younger pilots in our squadron. A strange feeling overshadowed me. The training that had just been completed had instilled confidence in my flying abilities and a secret desire to prove myself in battle. It was a mixed feeling. A feeling of confidence accompanied by a feeling that made you ask yourself if you were as good as you thought you were. That thought would be pushed aside and once again replaced with the assurance that you were good. After all, US

Navy pilots were reported to be the best pilots in the world, and you were a Navy pilot. You knew that you had to keep that thought. If you went into battle thinking your opponent was better than you, your confidence level would be low. If your confidence level is low, your ability would also suffer and put you at a disadvantage.

Never allow yourself to think you could be killed. Fear of death is like a curse and will, without a doubt, increase your chance of failure and diminish your performance. If you go in thinking you are the best, you will have a much better chance of doing your best. A wave of anxiety swept through our ranks.

F9F-6 Cougar. Taken by Sam Hubbard.

Wayne Fox (left) and Bill Russ (middle) in our gun tub.

CHAPTER II

BACK TO THE BEGINNING

I started to think about home, my parents, and my sister. I thought about my other six buddies who joined the navy with me at the same time. We were from a little town in Iowa named Sumner, with a population of about 2,000. It was the only place in the world for us. We had joined as enlisted men and would take our boot training in San Diego, California. This was to take place in early January.

That day arrived. The local paper had to take our picture and publish it in the Sumner Gazette. Seven young men leaving a small town was big news.

We joined a troop train heading for California. This, in itself, was an adventure. None of us had ever been away from home for an extended period, and certainly not heading for a destination 2,000 miles away and being gone for four years.

The troop train had a club car on it with a bar. This was more than a temptation; it was a challenge to see if we could buy a drink. Most of us were 19 years old and looked our age. Nevertheless, we had to try. I was trying to think how I could act older to be more convincing to the bartender. Finally, I settled on ordering a drink that would establish me as someone more mature. My choice became a martini. Now, I had never had a martini and had no idea how it was made or what it would taste like. I don't think I had ever tasted gin in the past. Surprisingly, my age was not questioned, and I was presented with my martini, olive, and all. After walking over to the table where my friends were, I sat down and eyed my martini, wondering what I had. I finally summoned up enough courage to try it. I don't know how I got that first sip down. I was convinced I had been given hair oil to drink.

How I ever drank that thing, I am not sure. I just knew that my friends were watching. The bartender was also watching, along with the entire world. I had to drink it or lose face. Somehow, I managed to drink it. I don't know how I did, but I drank it.

Our troop train arrived in San Diego in the night. We disembarked, were loaded into a bus, and driven to the base. Our processing started immediately. This lasted well into the night and early morning. We finally arrived at our barracks with dawn not too far away. At six in the morning, we were awakened with revelry and welcomed to our new home by the Chief that would be our leader for the next few weeks. This was Chief Ellis.

Chief Ellis assigned me to guard duty in front of our barracks. I was not sure what I was guarding. Must have been the clothesline, because that was all we had in front of our quarters that seemed to have the only value within miles.

I diligently assumed my role as the protector of the clothesline. I am not sure how I was supposed to defend the clothesline. I only had a short piece of wood that resembled a broom handle. If I were attacked, I was not sure what I would do with it. If I hit my assailant with it, I am sure it would only increase his anger and make him more aggressive. I finally saw a stranger approaching. Immediately I assumed my fighting stance in an effort to portray a vicious, well-trained clothesline guard. As he approached, I took note of his size. If he got down on his knees, I think I would still have to look up to him. I was not sure if I should run screaming fire to arouse my fellow sleeping clothesline guards or stand my ground. The decision was quickly decided when I found my legs didn't work and I could not even walk fast, let alone run.

This hulk of a man stopped directly in front of me and blared out. "Sailor, what is the fifth general order?"

I came back with a snappy reply. "What are general orders?" I discovered immediately that was not the answer he was looking for. He quickly produced a notepad and pencil.

"What is your name and company number, Sailor?"

I knew what that was, so I came to attention and promptly answered him. For the next ten minutes, I received a very informative lecture on general orders. It ended with him telling me to report for KP duty at 0500 hours the next morning. Needless to say, I was not overjoyed with what he said. He added, "The next time I ask you for general orders you better know every one of them forward and backward. Is that clear?"

That was my first experience as a clothesline guard and the value of knowing what general orders are. He did leave a lasting impression.

After this initial encounter with this Navy Chief, boot camp was not that bad. We had a great bunch of men that were just like me. Everyone was away from home, many for the first time and all in need of friends. We quickly became acquainted and good pals.

After boot camp, we all went our separate ways. None of the men that joined with me were allowed to stay together. I don't recall seeing any of my hometown friends while serving at an active duty station. We saw each other again on leave, but not there.

We had an interview just before leaving boot camp to determine what we wanted to do in the Navy. I had just turned 19 and did not have a clue what I wanted to do, so I told the interviewer I would like to be assigned sea duty and strike for a gunner's mate.

Somehow, I had gotten a very perceptive man for my interview. He told me I had very high scores on my IQ test and suggested I try for pilot training. It sounded like a new adventure to me, and one I would like to pursue. I did not understand what it entailed, but I eagerly accepted his proposal and was held over at boot camp until I could report to another base for further testing. After this was completed, I was assigned to a photo squadron for a short time without knowing how my tests had gone. From the photo squadron, I was sent to the Aviation Machinist Mates School in Jacksonville, Florida. Just before my graduation, I received word that I had been accepted for pilot training. I received orders to report to Pensacola, Florida as soon as I graduated from the mechanic's school.

I reported to Pensacola in early October and was sworn into the Aviation Cadet program on October 12, 1951, my 20th birthday. I immediately started ground school.

I did not have an optimistic outlook on the outcome I envisioned for myself as a cadet. Most of the entire group of new cadets had at least two years of college, and many had more. On the other hand, I did not have any college at all. I felt that I would not be able to compete with the other men. I hoped that I would at least be able to fly a Navy plane a few times.

Preflight school lasted three months. I was amazed to find myself in the top half of my class, which gave me the confidence I had lacked at the beginning. From preflight, I reported to NAS Whiting Field for my first hands-on experience with an airplane. Lt. Rannie was to be my first flight instructor. I would fly the SNJ trainer. Flying came easy for me, I felt at home while I was flying. Lt. Rannie thought I had some experience in flying before I joined the Navy. I assured him I did not. We were moved from one field to another to learn how to be a Navy pilot. One field might be for formation flying, another may be for learning to fly.

The final phase of our basic training was to learn how to land on an aircraft carrier. This was the most trying of all the segments of flying. This final part of our training ended with qualifying on the aircraft carrier USS Monterey. We had to make six landings before we could move on. I qualified the first time by making six landings in six passes. I did not receive any pilot-caused wave-offs.

From Pensacola, I was sent to Kingsville, Texas to complete my advanced training. We would either fly the F6F Hellcat fighter or the F8F Bearcat fighter in the initial segment of our advanced training. The F8F was considered one of the top performing fighters of all time. I had the honor of being assigned to fly the F8F. Everyone finished in the F6F because of some structural flaws in the F8F. That meant the final two stages of advanced training, gunnery, and carrier qualification would be done in the F6F by all the cadets.

The F8F had never seen combat in WWII because it had arrived too late. This airplane can only be described as awesome. It was designed to combat the Japanese Kamikazes. In 1946, it set a climbing record that it held for many years. After a takeoff run of only 115 feet, it was at 10,000 feet in 94 seconds. It was the only airplane I ever flew that I could not adjust the seat or unlock my shoulder straps. The cockpit was so small you could touch everything without doing so. It had an R2800 radial engine with 2,000 horsepower. Your feet were in two holes that led to the rudder pedals. I remember that we also sat on a 185-gallon gas tank. Our instructor also told us he never knew of anyone that survived a bailout in the F8F. Because of its size, it was impossible to avoid hitting the tail in a bailout. We were told the only chance we had was to roll on our back and release our seat belt trying to drop out. It would still be questionable if you would miss the tail. Many pilots lost their lives in the F8F. It was truly an awesome plane. Because of its immense power, it could be very dangerous for an inexperienced pilot. It was the cause of many fatalities in training cadets. My roommate, Don Jackson, died in it along with another classmate, Don Becker, when they had a midair collision while night flying.

The final stage of Advanced Training was to make eight carrier landings in the F6F. I, again, was fortunate to make eight landings in eight passes with no wave-offs. I was allowed to fly one of the F6Fs back to the base. The other students had to spend hours riding the Monterey back. My plane happened to be one of the front planes that would take off from the carrier, so I received my first catapult shot. I did, however, receive the catapult shot before I was ready. Someone pushed the button too soon. This could have had some terrible results, but I was able to gain control by the time I reached the end of the deck. Fortunately, I had the engine at full throttle, but I was not braced for the early shot that came too soon. The acceleration is so great that if you are not ready, it is almost impossible to get hold of the controls before you reach the end of the flight deck. Luckily, I had the plane trimmed for flight.

I finished my flight training and received my commission and wings in March 1953. I was 21 years old at the time. It was a very proud day for me. I can still see the smile on my mother's face as she pinned my wings on me. I went home to Iowa with my parents for a short leave with orders to report to the All-Weather School, followed by Jet School. While I was at home, the war in Korea ended. I had a standing joke that the enemy must have heard I was on my way, so they just ended the war.

After my leave ended, I reported back to Pensacola and finished the two remaining schools, which were All-Weather School and Jet School. I had the opportunity, while in jet school, to fly the first Air Force jet fighter. That was the F-80 Shooting Star. This was a step back in history. From there, I received orders to VF-91 in Alameda, California. The squadron I was joining had just returned from the war in Korea. The pilots were a grand and colorful group, which included two Aces from WWII. Most of them would receive assignments to other duties or squadrons before we started our training. We trained for about nine months, losing one of our 31 pilots to an accident involving the flying tail.

After I joined the squadron VF-91, we had a period of adjustment. It included getting to know each other, and even more important, learning to trust each other. Sam told me once that the Skipper must have enjoyed being around young pilots because there were so many of us.

I remember when I first joined VF-91 in California. As mentioned, I had met Sam Hubbard while in training, so we knew each other and eventually shared a suite of rooms in the Bachelor Officers' Quarters on the base. Sam was the only one I recognized; everyone else was a stranger. I don't know who recognized who first, but I believe both of us were happy to see at least one friendly face. I checked into the squadron and thought I had better meet my new Skipper, so I made my way to the Skipper's office. As I nervously raised my hand to knock on the door, I nearly hit Sam in the head as the door opened suddenly. He had just paid his respects to the Skipper and was leaving. We just looked at each other for a moment and started to laugh. I don't know if we thought what happened was funny or just because we saw someone we knew. I knew, at that moment, somehow a relationship was formed, a bond that could never be broken. I am not sure how you can understand something like that, but it is just something you know. "Foxy, are you trying to pound on me? It is Foxy, isn't it?"

"If you're Sam, I can't think of anyone I would rather pound on. As bad a pilot as you are, I thought they washed you out a long time ago. They must be getting desperate."

Sam replied. "I can fly circles around you anytime."

"Sam, I'm going to pay my respects to the Skipper. Want to meet me at the club in about an hour for a beer?"

"Sounds good. I'm going to the BOQ (Bachelor Officers Quarters) to check on my room to see if I have been assigned a roommate. You got anyone yet?"

"Not that I know of. I just arrived here yesterday. Maybe, if you care to, we can see if we can bunk together."

"I think that would work since we already know each other. My setup, where I am now, is two separate bedrooms, a living room, and a shared bath. I think all the quarters are that way. I'll check on it and get it going. We can decide which place we want to live in and make a move as soon as we can."

"That should work out fine. I'll see you at the club later. You can let me know what happened then." With that, Sam left. I was pleased because Sam appeared to be a great guy and had a lot on the ball.

I turned and knocked on the door that read, "Commanding Officer."

"Come in!" Thundered a voice from the other side of the door. I was a bit nervous as I opened the door and briskly walked to the desk where the Skipper was seated. I offered my best salute, which he returned with one much more relaxed.

"Ensign Fox, reporting for duty, Sir."

With that, he rose from his chair with a stern face and offered a welcome to Fighter Squadron 91. As he stood up, he extended his hand, which I grasped firmly and shook. We enjoyed a pleasant conversation with the Skipper asking a lot of questions about my family and background. He also asked if I had a preference for my collateral duty that we held in the squadron in addition to flying. At one point, I inquired about a picture he had on the wall that showed a burning plane passing over the fantail of an aircraft carrier. He told me that was a Kamikaze that had just been hit before it reached the ship. He also said he was the LSO (landing signal officer) and was on the fantail at that time and could feel the heat of the burning plane as it passed over him.

We concluded the meeting and shook hands once again. I then left the room and started for the officers' quarters.

I had some extra time and wanted to see if Sam was still there and if he was able to get the rooms switched. I was told he had just left, and they were rearranging it so we could share our living quarters. I was also given some mail that had preceded me. Most were the usual, like mail from my parents and sister. There was one that stood out from the others. It was from Mary Beth Counter. Mary Beth had married my best friend from advanced training, who was Jerry Counter. Jerry and I were inseparable throughout advanced training, Jet School, and All-Weather School. He had been assigned to a squadron in Miramar, California, which was flying F9F-5 Panther jets. I had been home with Jerry and met his family and wife-to-be, Mary Beth. I was curious why the letter was from Mary Beth and not Jerry. Pushing all thoughts aside, I quickly opened it and read its contents. Mary Beth came right to the point and told me Jerry had been killed. He was taking off from Miramar. As he climbed out, the airplane exploded, giving Jerry no chance to eject.

I felt a cold chill go up my back. I just sat down, overcome with emotions, and tried to hold back the tears, but I had little success. Jerry and I had shared so much of our lives and had become very close. It brought back memories of the good times and reminded me of Bob Olsen, who lived across from us in advanced training. Bob often accompanied Jerry and me on our adventures, or perhaps misadventures. He would jokingly call Jerry Lunch Counter and me Sly Fox. Bob was a great golfer and had placed well in the Corpus Christi golf open. He told us he was thinking about quitting the flight program before we went back to Pensacola for our final carrier qualifications. We told him that was foolish. All he had to do was make eight landings on an aircraft carrier with the F6F Hellcat fighter before getting his wings and commission. I think Bob must have had a premonition of his death because he lost his life a little later in jet school when he flew into a hill on a low altitude rendezvous.

Don Jackson again made an entrance into my thoughts. Don was also a roommate, as I mentioned before, in advanced training with Jerry and me. He and another of our roommates, C. D. Hill, and a classmate Don Becker were on a night flying hop. Hill later told us they were doing breakup and rendezvous. Hill had managed to join up with the leader, but Jackson and Becker failed to appear. He then saw two flashes on the ground. One of them had broken too soon and crashed into the other plane. Both lost their lives.

I am sure I know what happened. The instructor who was with them was a Marine first lieutenant who we had an encounter with earlier. Three of us cadets were walking by a hangar when we met the Lieutenant. There are many officers at an airbase, so it was a custom not to salute. We did not salute him, so he stopped us and chewed us out severely. He was overly impressed with his authority and was eager to display it. I am sure he was very adamant and critical of my roommates' performance the night of the accident and was displaying it profusely. I feel he had the men so rattled that they were not able to think. That is only my opinion. He was required to seal up Don's locker the next day. He just kept repeating that he wished he could bring both of the men who died back to life.

This meant that in advance training, two of my three roommates died and also two other friends. I am not sure what happened to the third man who was the last of my roommates. I lost track of him and never saw him again. Our class was not very large, so this was difficult to accept. Of the three of us I could account for, I was the only one that survived.

In preflight we had a similar situation. I had five roommates. Two I lost track of. Of the remaining three, I am sure of one being killed and was told another was as well. The remaining roommate was an exchange student from France. He was in a bad accident and, I believe, he never flew again. I was also in a very serious accident that I was injured in but returned to flying. Of the three accounted for roommates and me, I was the only one that continued to fly.

While in the Navy, I was in six accidents. One, of which, I should not have survived and received injuries. Two of the others could have gone either way.

I glanced at my watch and saw I was already late meeting Sam, so I headed to the Officer's Club.

F6F Hellcat.

F8F Bearcat.

SNJ training airplane (Plane I learned to fly in).

T-34 Training plane

CHAPTER III

MEET THE FAMILY

I found Sam seated in the club at a table in the corner of the room with three other officers. As I was looking around, Sam raised his hand and quietly yelled, "Foxy." I had already seen him, so I was starting in that direction. When I reached the table, Sam pushed out a chair with his foot and told me to have a seat. As I did, he said, "I want you to meet some other pilots that will be flying with us in 91." He continued, "This is Jim Hargrove, Lee Pritcher, and Chuck Adams. Jim and Lee are new like us; Chuck was with the old squadron and will leave when he is reassigned." I shook hands with them and told them it was nice to meet them, which they echoed back.

Jim looked at me and said, "Where you from, Foxy?"

"I'm from Iowa, where the tall corn grows. Where you from?"

"I'm from Texas, where the longhorn cattle grow." With that, we all got a chuckle. Lee was from the Midwest, and Chuck was from Oregon.

Chuck started fielding questions from all of us who wanted to know all about the cruise he had just returned from. Chuck had seen a lot of combat and did not mind embellishing on it as he related it to us. Lee and Jim were Ensigns just out of training like Sam and me. Chuck was a Ltjg. (Lieutenant junior grade).

As the afternoon went on, more officers came in for a drink to soften the memories of a toilsome day. At least, that always sounded like a good excuse. A tall, lanky LCDR (Lieutenant Commander) walked directly over to our table. Looking at Chuck he said, "Hi, Chuck, who are your friends?"

Chuck answered, "Some of your new pilots that are just joining VF-91." He then introduced us to Lieutenant Commander Ed Hitchcock, who was the new executive officer that would be with us on this cruise.

"Nice to meet you, gentlemen. I am looking forward to getting to know you all better. We have a great new airplane that should be very interesting to fly. By the way, The Skipper has scheduled an 0800 meeting for all pilots in the morning. Pass the word to the other guys. Anyway, enough business, mind if I join you?"

Everyone offered an affirmative answer, eager to accommodate our new Executive Officer.

Chuck spotted some previous members of VF-91 and invited them to join us. Several other pilots overheard our conversation and joined us. They introduced themselves as new members of VF-91 and were eager to get acquainted. We would go to sea with 31 pilots. It seemed like most of them were at the club.

Our little get-together lasted a little longer than expected, but it started to break up in a couple of hours. I think the married guys left first. I believe they had to report to their Skipper at home. Jerry was still on my mind, and I wanted to spend a little quiet time. I told Sam I was tired and would meet him for breakfast in the morning and to call me when he was ready to go. I had some lunch meat in my refrigerator back in my room that I would make do for my supper. I just needed to be alone for a while.

I think pilots treat the death of a friend differently than other folks. They may dwell on their lost friend for a few days. After this, they rarely mentioned his name. His memory was parked in the corner of their mind but never forgotten. I think perhaps they just don't want to let themselves believe it could happen to them. If they don't talk about him, they can trick themselves into thinking it never happened. I guess you could say it is a denial response.

The next morning dawned bright and clear, appearing to say that we had a new start to the rest of our life. Everything up to that point was history and couldn't be changed, but the future was before us, and we are the master of what we do with it.

If we put our faith in God and seek His help, there is nothing we can't accomplish. That's why I always start the day asking God to guide me through the day. I thought of Jerry again, and his wife and family. Sometimes God has different plans for what we envisioned for ourselves. Sometimes it was hard to understand and even harder to accept. It was, however, his plan and one that takes precedence. I believe everything happens for a reason. We may never know why while we occupy our allotted space on Earth.

There was a knock on the door, so I just said: "Come in." It was Sam.

"Ready for breakfast?" He asked.

"I'm bright-eyed, bushy-tailed, and ready to meet the challenges of the day."

"That fits you good with your last name, but I'll just say that I'm bright-eyed and ready for the day. I think yesterday we met a lot of the men we'll be flying with in the future. They all look good to me."

I agreed, so we went to breakfast and on to the hanger our squadron occupied.

It was interesting to meet the other members of VF-91, both the new and those from the old squadron. Some pilots from the old squadron were veterans from WWII. Two of them were Aces (had shot down five or more enemy planes), and one other had been a prisoner of the Germans. Hugh Batten was returning from an airstrike while fighting the Japanese. The ship had Jap Kamikazes on the radar, but the CAP (Combat Air Patrol) could not get to them in time. Hugh requested permission to intercept them, which was eagerly granted. On his first pass, he shot down four of the enemy planes. He got his fifth later. Herman Fouche was in the European theater. It was said he went right into the landing pattern at a German airfield and would come up behind one plane, shoot him down, and move on to the next. He was receiving heavy gunfire from the ground, but it did not deter him. One of the other pilots, by the name of Turnbull, had been taken prisoner by the Germans. He was befriended by a German guard who, more than once, pulled him out of a line of prisoners to be shot. He was still corresponding with that guard.

We also had a pilot, Gordon Gray, who had held the world aircraft speed record for a time. They were all very impressive.

The Skipper, Commander Red Voltz, made his appearance, and all came to attention. As he walked to the front of the room, he gave the command to be at ease and be seated. He then welcomed us all to VF-91 and summed up what he expected from us. Loyalty, dedication, and discipline. He placed a particular emphasis on following orders, especially in the air. He told us our life, and the lives of the other pilots could depend on that and further related that there was zero tolerance on this. Those who did not follow this rule would be dealt with harshly.

It was a friendly meeting that left no doubt who was in charge. We would fly with different experienced pilots, so the senior pilots could choose who they wanted in their flight. We had several Panther jets that we could fly now but expected our Cougars within a week. He told us to stay in our hangar and get acquainted. He wanted to have the senior pilots get to know the younger pilots. He also said we would start flying the next day, so be sure to check the flight schedule later. All came to attention as he left the room. The rest of the day was spent just getting to know each other.

Sam and I walked out to the Panther jets to have a good look at them. Neither of us had ever flown one before. We also picked up a handbook to learn more about them since there would be instructions and cockpit checkouts to become familiar with the Panther. The cockpit checks were scheduled to start later today. One thing I was happy about was that the Panther and Cougar had very similar cockpits.

The next few days were routine, although we flew the Panthers a few times. Our Cougars, all twenty of them, came in and were being checked out and readied to fly. We were all excited about flying the Cougar, mainly because it could break the sound barrier. We were the second squadron in the Navy to fly the Cougar; a magnificent looking bird with its swept wings and sleek look. We would not carry bombs or rockets, just 20MM cannons. The Cougar was built for dogfighting.

We received a dispatch that said there was a problem with the flying tail. I touched on this earlier, but I believe it needs more clarification. The horizontal stabilizer and elevator could be locked together and function entirely as an elevator. The elevator is controlled by the back-and-forth movement of the stick, controlling the up and down motion or pitch of the nose. We were able to control the tail by turning it off or on with a switch in the cockpit. The flying tail gave us the ability to make a very sharp turn.

The Cougar did not have a standard aileron either. Ailerons are usually located on the trailing edge of each wing and controlled by the side-to-side movement of the stick. They controlled the lateral movement or roll of the airplane. The conventional ailerons on the Cougar had been replaced with air spoilers on top of the wings that were hydraulically operated.

As stated, we had received notice that the flying tail could run away and go to full up or full down, causing you to lose control of the airplane. We learned that the first squadron had to learn this the hard way. We were told they lost several of their thirty-one pilots when this occurred. I heard the number was seven, but this would be very high, so it was something I did not care to verify. It is possible, but even one pilot lost would have been too many. The use of the flying tail was restricted to over 10,000 feet. Our experience with supersonic jet fighters was about to begin.

At twenty-one years old, I was oblivious to any danger they might have posed. The learning period had just begun, with some lessons being learned the hard way. I know I had truly matured a lot since I joined the Navy when I was nineteen years old. I was now at twenty-one and thinking I was one of the Navy's top fighter pilots. There is an old saying that pride goes before a fall.

On one of the first days I flew the Cougar, I was scheduled to fly wing on Lt. Batten. It would be just the two of us. I stood in awe of Lt. Batten since he was an Ace, and that can only command respect. We made a section (formation) take off, rolling together side by side on the runway, and climbed to 20,000 feet. We did a few turns to get the feel of the planes. I was flying a loose formation position, which we practiced on a typical flight like this. It is called a fluid position and allows the wingman to slip from side to side to hold the most advantageous combat position.

The fluid formation also extends to a four man formation as well. The leader's wingman is free to slip from side to side as mentioned earlier. Also, the section leader and his wingman are fluid. The section leader, or the number three man in the formation and his wingman, is a team within a team. His wingman is free to slide back and forth on him, and he is free to slip back and forth on the leader and his wingman. If everyone stays loose and is free to move in a fluid position, the entire formation is much more flexible. The leader has the flexibility of making more abrupt maneuvers without concern of his wingman being in the way. The wingman's job is to keep the leader clear of any enemy aircraft. The section leader's wingman has the same job for the section leader. The section leader and his wingman can also fight as a team, with his wingman being the other part of his team. This has been found to be an effective way to fight. The leader of each of the two teams can concentrate on his target as his wingman keeps him clear.

All that has changed with the introduction of heat-seeking missiles. It is now possible that you will never see your target. It could be a long way out and not visible to the naked eye. You could be shooting at a dot on a scope.

Lt. Batten looked over at me and patted his right shoulder with his left hand, which told me to move in close and fly a tight position. Without warning, he started his nose up into a climbing turn to the left. At the ninety degrees position, we were inverted, on our backs, and continuing the ark below the horizon, returning to the level position. We had just done a barrel roll while flying in formation. I think he just wanted to see how good I was. I would have liked to have had some warning, but he wanted to see how I would react. I considered it an honor to fly wing with a man like Lt. Batten.

Sam and I did not usually fly together. We would both have to serve our time as a wingman. It's the learning curve all new Navy pilots must go through. It is required to prove yourself at one level before assuming the next.

For some unknown reason, Chuck Adams took a liking to me. I flew on his wing most of the time. We had given him a new handle, Squirrely. This was very fitting since you could never guess what he might do. I recall the time when it was just the two of us on a routine hop. We would make a section take-off as usual. It was customary in a formation take-off for the wingman to get slightly above the leader after they break free of the runway and drop down below him after they had gained some altitude. On this occasion, Chuck told me to stay stepped up on him. In other words, to stay slightly above him. I never questioned him; I just told him, OK. As we broke free of the runway, Squirrely gained minimal altitude above the treetop level and held it. We took off facing north and slowly came around to the south, remaining very low. I suddenly realized what he was up to. We were heading toward Mills College and passed over it extremely low and at full throttle. We were both dating girls that attended Mills College. According to them, when we talked to them later, we shook the entire school. It was a serious offense that could put us in a lot of hot water. However, we never heard anything about it from anyone in authority.

I was telling Sam about it sometime later when he relayed his tale to me about what they had done. Sam said, "Droopy Thomas and I went up to 40,000 feet and decided to go through the sound barrier." The Cougar would act rather strangely as it approached the sound barrier and tried to penetrate it. The stick would freeze and could not be moved until you had the shock wave past the wing spoilers and elevator. While it was doing this, the plane could roll to one side or the other. When this happened, control was lost temporarily, and you had to let it go wherever it wanted to.

Sam continued, "When the airplane rolled, and before I could get control, it rolled towards San Francisco, pointing us right at the city. We reduced throttle, but I knew the shockwave would hit the city. The Skipper was there to meet us when we landed and asked if we had broken the sound barrier. I couldn't lie, so I told him what happened. He said that the base had received a report that some big windows on Market street were broken. I have heard nothing more, but I suppose the Navy will have to pay for them."

I had to laugh and said, "At least you and Droopy shouldn't get into any trouble. You lost control of the plane which is normal. We could get our rear ends in a lot of hot water if someone reported us."

As we were continuing our conversation, the Skipper came into the ready room with a very troubled look on his face. He said, "Listen up, everyone. We just had one of our planes go into San Francisco Bay. It was on the other side of the Bay

Bridge. The chopper is heading to the crash site now, but we still don't have any firm reports, so we don't know if the pilot was able to get out. It was Belknap. It doesn't look good; he was too low to eject. He was on Goslow's wing. Goslow said Belknap pitched up and stalled. He got some control back, but pitched up again, stalled, and went into the bay. The plane either blew up or disintegrated. Goslow couldn't see it when it went into the water, but it had to be the flying tail from the information so far. He must have forgotten to make sure it was turned off. I'll let you know when I find anything out." He left the ready room after that and started back to his office. Many of our pilots were in the ready room. An eerie silence prevailed.

It must have been an hour before the Skipper returned. When he stepped into the room, he did not have to say anything as his face said it all. He hesitated, then said, "The only thing the chopper found was part of a Mae West and part of the headrest. He did not survive. We have secured all flight operations until further notice."

It was quiet as everyone left the ready room. Belknap was an Ensign in his early twenties. So much life would go unspent.

CDR. Voltz. The Skipper.

CHAPTER IV

LIFE GOES ON

Our flights continued but were perhaps tainted by what had happened. One would not be human if he could ignore what had taken place. We fought it the only way we knew how, and that was not to talk about it; to pretend it never happened or pretend it was a dream. The only one we had to convince was ourselves. You could never get calloused enough to ignore the loss of a friend. I do not know what motivated this, but I know it was the glue that held us together so we could still perform our job.

Sam and I talked about this. Even at this early stage in our flying career, we had witnessed this more than we cared to recall. Somehow, I think we conditioned ourselves into thinking we were impervious to such a fate, and it would only happen to someone else.

It was now time to continue with our training, so we were back to the grindstone trying to hone ourselves into proficient aerial gunners. We went to Fallon, Nevada, for weapons training. Since we were fighter pilots, our training would be concentrated on aerial gunnery and some ground strafing. Aerial gunnery consisted of one of us pulling a sleeve behind our airplane and the others making gunnery runs, firing live ammunition at it. The rounds would have paint on them with a different color for each pilot. When they passed through the cloth sleeve, they would leave paint on the cloth, making it possible to tell who fired the round.

Even though we had four 20MM cannons, we only fired two at a time to conserve ammunition. Sometimes someone would come in at a lower deflection angle than they should, so it was not uncommon to see tracers go by your wing closer than you liked.

I recall, on one occasion, we had climbed to 20,000 feet to start our gunnery runs. We practiced at about 20,000 feet instead of higher, such as 40,000 feet, because our planes would maneuver better in the denser air at 20,000 feet. We still had some fuel in our wing tanks, which could make the plane unstable in a tight turn. We decided to make some easy non-firing runs to use up the excess fuel. I rolled into a run and pulled too hard for that configuration. As a result, the plane immediately snapped into a stall and started to spin. The fuel in the wings acted like counterweights, which caused a very aggravated and violent spin. I tried for almost 10,000 feet to recover, but I was not successful. We had been informed if we were still in a spin under 10,000 feet, recovery might be extremely difficult or impossible.

As I approached 10,000 feet, I made several attempts to blow the canopy off and eject, but I was thrown around so badly I could not get hold of the lever to blow the canopy. I had one option left, and that was to blow myself through the canopy, but this was extremely risky since you would have to pass by the sharp edges of the shattered canopy. I had known of one pilot who was successful in doing this.

I released my hold on the stick and was trying desperately to arm the seat, which was difficult to do. I had to arm the seat before I could activate it. When I let go of all the controls while trying to arm the seat, the plane recovered by itself and assumed a shallow dive. I did not look at the altitude since I was too busy, but I feel sure I was below 10,000 feet. I climbed back and continued our gunnery. I will always think I had some help on this one. If it was divine help, I am very grateful.

As you can imagine, Fallon provided lots of entertainment with its gambling and, of course, the young ladies who frequented these establishments. Sam and I often partook of this welcomed entertainment. One evening, I had strolled away from Sam in the quest to make my fortune. After not being successful, I journeyed back to where Sam was seated at a table. "Hey, Sam, you ready to move on to greener pastures?" It was then that I noticed Sam was not gambling.

"Think I may stick it out here. I may be able to learn something."

"How can you learn something when you're not playing, and no one else is either?"

"Depends on what you want to learn."

My gaze drifted over to the young lady who was the dealer. She was quite attractive and wearing a bright smile. "Have you got a friend?" I asked the young lady. "Or you can dump Sam, and I'll take you to dinner."

"Hey! I got here first. She has already agreed to get a bite to eat with me."

The young lady smiled and said, "Maybe I can find one of my friends who would like to go along."

I smiled in return and said, "If she is as nice as you, I think that may work. If not, consider my first offer."

"I get off in about 10 minutes; want to come back then?"

"Sounds like a date; we'll be back," Sam offered.

We walked around a bit and came back within our allotted ten minutes. The young lady kept her promise and was accompanied by an attractive friend. We went out and ended up having a great time. The time came to take them home. I had my car, so I was driving, and Sam was in the back seat with his young lady. As we were driving along, I heard a loud crack followed by an angry, "That is not supposed to be patted and pinched, it is supposed to be cuddled and loved." The crack was a very well-directed slap on the cheek of an overly ambitious Sam. The ride to where they lived was rather quiet after that. I received a friendly kiss goodnight. I am not sure how Sam fared. He never would tell me if she got over it, and we never saw them again.

As mentioned before, I often flew with Squirrely Adams, who continued to live up to his name. One day after gunnery practice, Squirrely told me he would like to get a look at Lake Tahoe. It was late in the day and would be getting dark soon, but I thought it was a good idea too. We flew over the lake until we reached the north end. Adams said he wanted to get a better look at the lake, so we started letting down. Then we came around to the south while still descending. At about a hundred feet, he leveled off and advanced the throttle to increase our speed. From there, he went even lower. I did not look at my airspeed indicator, but I knew we had to be over 500 miles per hour and still accelerating. We usually spoke in terms of knots per hour. I was using miles per hour, which was higher.

When we were reaching the end of the lake, I could see buildings coming up, which was a gambling resort. We passed over the resort at an extremely low altitude and pulled up sharply to go over a small mountain. I did glance at my mach needle (registers the speed in relation to the percentage of the speed of sound), which was indicating over .8. That was over 600 miles per hour. I said later that I bet every slot machine in the place must have paid off since I was sure we shook the building down to its foundation.

Quite often, some of us might go back from Fallon to Alameda for the evening for some reason or another. The Skipper was going back this day, so three of us tagged along with him. Before we left, he said we should expect to hit some weather over Alameda so we might be on instruments. He didn't miss that call. We hit some extremely bad weather with heavy rainstorms. We tried to come over the runway in an echelon to break up and land. Every time we did, we broke out of the clouds, but we would go right back in them, making it impossible to land. After completing several failed attempts, the tower called and said the base just received a call that we had knocked some TV antennas off a house in Oakland. Oakland is the city in California where Alameda Naval Air Station is located. This was very unlikely since we did not go that low. We would be in trouble now if we did not get on the ground soon. I was not sure we had enough fuel for each of us to make a separate instrument approach, and I was number four.

An instrument approach can be very time consuming. Ground control will have radio control of you as soon as you are in their airspace. They can only take one plane at a time for an instrument approach, so each plane must hold until the plane before him has landed. This procedure would continue until all four planes are on the ground. Ground control will bring you to the field and at some point, turn you over to Approach Control. Approach Control will talk to you as you enter the landing sequence. When you start your final approach, you cannot answer the approach control operator. They will talk constantly to you. They will start you on a glideslope to contact the runway in the proper place. They will tell you if you are on the glideslope, above or below it. You must make corrections as they give them to you. If you don't hear them, you probably have lost radio contact with them and must abort the approach. They can bring you right down to the runway, but this was only for very experienced pilots.

I have been in an approach with a friend when there was so much electricity in the air, they would lose radio contact with us almost at the last second, we would have to abort the landing and try again. In this case, we were finally sent out and told to hold our position by flying on a range leg over the Gulf Of Mexico. That was one of the roughest rides I have ever had in an airplane.

On our way back to Pensacola, we were advised not to continue when we landed at New Orleans for fuel. My friend had the highest instrument rating the Navy had, so we continued. After taking off and about halfway to Pensacola, we hit a violent storm. It was raining so hard; our engine temperature fell below the take-off minimum. At Pensacola, each instrument approach ended in their losing us on the radar. This is when we were sent out to sea to hold. The storm was so violent that we were being thrown all over the sky. At one point we must have dropped close to 300 feet in a downdraft. The weather finally cleared, making it possible for us to land.

In the above case, we had been to an Airforce base in Texas to obtain some Airforce flight helmets. We had gone into Mexico and purchased a lot of liquor and had it stored in the belly of the plane. I knew it would all be broken, but when we looked, we never broke a bottle.

Back to Alameda. There was some hesitation after we were told we had knocked some TV antennas off a house. The Skipper called Alameda tower and said, "This is Junegrass one, coming in low over Oakland." He was leaving no doubt about what he was going to do.

It was difficult to see the runway with all the rain, so the Skipper came in low enough for all of us to make our break and start our landing pattern. As soon as I hit the runway, I began to hydroplane, We were on one of the shortest runways at Alameda, so I had to get stopped. It was just like I was on ice. I started to hit one rudder and then the other to make my plane skid sideways to get more air resistance and slow me down. We all made it OK.

CHAPTER V

THE UNEXPECTED

Sometimes something may happen that will make you question your sanity, or at least question what you are seeing. As pilots, we are conditioned to make quick appraisals of any situation and deal with them. However, that too can be unexpectedly put to the test.

As mentioned before, we would often fly back to Alameda for one reason or another. On this occasion, Squirrely Adams and I were sent back to Alameda to pick up some supplies. We would fly to Alameda after we were finished flying for the day at Fallon and return early the next morning. We would have a little extra time allotted to us. We could have a date that evening, or just go out for a while and do whatever we wanted to do.

It was just getting dark as we pulled onto the runway at Fallon. I was going to fly wing on Adams, and he would lead. However, before we taxied onto the runway to take off, he pointed to the side of his helmet at the ear position, then to his oxygen mask where the mic was located, and gave me a thumbs down to tell me he could not transmit. He then patted his head on top and pointed to me, which meant I was to take the lead. I acknowledged by patting my head and pointing to myself. By doing this, he knew I understood and had accepted the lead. I then taxied out ahead of him so he could get into position on my wing. When the leader is sure his wingman is in position, he will hold up his hand with two fingers extended and move his hand in a circular motion. This is telling his wingman to go to full power. The leader also goes to full power and pulls the throttle back slightly so the wingman will have a little extra power to stay in position when rolling. The leader will continue to hold his hand up. The wingman will then take one last look at his instruments to make sure the engine is operating as it should. After doing so, he will give the leader a thumbs up telling him he is ready. When the leader drops his hand, it is the signal to release the brakes. They will start to roll immediately. When the two planes reach flying speed, the wingman will move slightly higher than the leader after he leaves the runway. He has his eyes on the leader and not being able to look at the runway. He must do this so he will not accidentally make contact with the runway again. As they gain height, the wingman will drop back into a formation position. This is called a section or formation takeoff. The landing gear are raised at a signal from the leader.

After we were in the air, I set the throttle to climbing power and turned toward Alameda. We were only going a few hundred miles, so I only climbed high enough to clear the mountains. By the time we were getting close to Alameda, it was completely dark. I contacted the tower for landing instructions and was told to land on runway 36, which was in a northerly direction.

Runways are numbered by the compass direction they point in using only two numbers. In this case, the 36 would indicate a direction of 360 which is directly north. The same runway pointing the opposite direction would be to the south or runway 18.

I swung to the south of Alameda then turned back North to line up with the runway. When we were approaching Alameda, I signaled Adams to dump his wing fuel tanks. We always took off with all fuel tanks full, but with almost nine hundred gallons of jet fuel at five pounds to the gallon, we would be too heavy to land with these tanks full, so we dumped the wing tanks which held about a hundred gallons each. It was an interesting sight to see all that fuel stream out of the wingtips.

I started a high speed let down at about thirty miles out. As I was approaching Alameda, I noticed something out on my left wing flying formation with us. It looked sort of gray and kind of oval shaped. I quickly called Adams and asked what was on my left wing. He still could hear me but was unable to talk to me. I was between the object and Adams, so he had to drop down to try to see what it was. When he did, the object accelerated ahead at a tremendous speed. I was going about 300 miles an hour or possibly faster, so his speed had to be off the charts. Adams was not able to see it because it moved away at such a rapid speed. At first, I thought it could have been a reflection between my canopy and Adam's canopy, but this object moved straight ahead. A reflection would have followed the curvature of my canopy. I was visibly shaken. There was no question in my mind that we had something join on us for a short time. UFOs were not as much of an issue back in 1953 as they are today.

When we landed and went into the hanger, the Skipper was there, so I told him what I had seen. He laughed and told me not to tell anyone as they would think I was crazy. Later, a dispatch came out directing pilots to report such sightings. There must have been other pilots who saw what I saw. In later years this became a big issue when many unidentified objects were sighted by pilots in California. We enjoyed an evening in Alameda and had an uneventful trip back to Fallon.

We continued our weapons training in Fallon until the Skipper thought all of us were ready for combat.

We would soon start our preparations for carrier qualifications, but until then, we continued to practice working together and getting to feel comfortable flying together. Mock dogfights were one of the ways we did this. Chuck Adams had been transferred to another squadron, so I had been adopted by Jack Snyder, who was a senior lieutenant and a flight leader. I was the number two man in his flight. Bear Kauffman was chosen to be the section leader with Jim Hargrove tail-end Charlie. Jack had seen a lot of action in Korea and had become an excellent and aggressive pilot. Bear had seen duty with another squadron, so he too was experienced. Jim was new like me and was an excellent pilot, but he had made a wheels-up landing while we were in Fallon.

I was walking out to my plane with the Skipper when I was the first one to see Jim landing. He was about to touch down with his wheels still in the up position. "He doesn't have his wheels down!" I yelled.

The Skipper whirled around and started shouting as if Jim could hear him. Just before he hit the runway, he must have realized his wheels were still in the up position and added full throttle. It was too late as his plane contacted the runway, and for a few seconds, was engulfed in flames. The fire quickly extinguished itself as he continued sliding down the runway. Jim could have gotten into a lot of hot water, but the Skipper knew he was a good pilot. He just made a mistake. Mistakes while flying can be costly and often fatal, so he was very fortunate.

Mechanical failures were not uncommon with such a sophisticated airplane as the Cougar. We continuously practiced emergencies, trying to prepare ourselves for anything we could possibly have to deal with. We also had backup systems to help us overcome any such emergency. I used to think we had backup systems for our backup systems.

On one occasion, I was happy that I had these backup systems. I was taking off from Alameda when I noticed my canopy was closing slowly. I had to help pull it shut. As we climbed out, I was flying with Jim Hargrove as my wingman, so I asked him to check the outside of my plane for anything unusual. He came over, pulled in close, and slowly slid from one side to the other. When he came up on the other side, he told me he thought I had a ruptured hydraulic line and had lost all my hydraulic fluid. I could now confirm this since my flaperons (lateral wing spoilers) were not functioning correctly. The emergency system had cut in with just half of the flaperons working, which were the flaperettes. My wheels had been able to retract to the full up position. I would have preferred that they had stayed in the down position because I was not sure I would be able to get them down and locked later. I had an air bottle that was supposed to do just that in an emergency. It wasn't long before I had a chance to find out if it was working.

I still had a full load of fuel, so I had to get rid of as much as I could. I climbed to 10,000 feet with Jim on my wing, dumping my wing tanks as I did. I would be too heavy to land with a full supply of fuel. As I said before, we carried about nine hundred gallons of fuel weighing close to five thousand pounds or about two-and-a-half tons. I wanted to burn up as much as I could before I attempted a landing.

I notified Alameda tower that I had an emergency. I knew I would need the full runway and the emergency arresting gear (cable on the runway with an anchor chain attached to it so the tailhook could pick it up and stop the airplane). The arresting gear could be a critical issue. Without it, I could end up in the bay. The tower informed me I would have to use runway 28. They also said that there was construction on the approach end with tall cranes just off the approach end. The runway was already short, so now it was necessary to come in high to avoid the cranes, and that was something I did not need. Runway 28 ran right up to the bay, so if I did not get stopped, I would end up in the water. Going into shallow water can be dangerous because an airplane can easily flip over and trap the pilot inside. I could not extend my flaps without hydraulics, so I would be landing at a higher speed and without brakes. That gives me a lot of comfort, I thought.

While I was burning up fuel, I started to prepare the airplane for landing. The landing gear had an emergency air bottle in the hydraulic system that was aimed at the landing gear. The air would give a sudden blast to the landing gear and hopefully force the gear down and in the locked position. There was no guarantee, however. I informed Jim what I was going to do and released the air into the system and held my breath as he checked them. He said they looked like they were in place, so I then lowered the tailhook and received a positive answer from Jim that it was down.

I called the tower and asked for clearance to land. When I received their reply that I was cleared to land, I thought if I did not pick up the arresting wire, I could go around and try again. I realized though that I could lose the use of my flaperettes and not be able to control the airplane laterally. I would be too low to eject, so this approach was a one-shot deal. I was heading north, so I started a slow turn to a heading of 28. I was not sure how long I would have the use of my flaperettes since they too were controlled by hydraulics. They did have an air bottle that I could release into their system similar to the landing gear. I could only get up to 21 movements of the stick before the air was exhausted. The flaperettes controlled my lateral (roll) movements, but I would also have some lateral control with my rudders. If one of my wings were going down, I could push the opposite rudder. This would put the airplane in a skid. While in a skid, the fuselage would block some of the air on the high wing. That decreases the airflow over that wing, and you will lose lift on the wing. The other wing will now have more lift so it will come up.

I elected to wait and release the air into the flaperettes as long as I could, and as long as I still was able to control the plane with my rudders. As I was about to reach the cranes, I released the air into the flaperette system. Even though I just cleared the cranes, I was still quite high, and without flaps, I had to land at a very high speed. I believe it was near 140 knots, which was over 160 miles per hour. As soon as I hit the runway, I was standing on the brakes, not sure if they had any effect at all. I think all I did was burn the brakes up. I felt the hook engage the wire and anchor chain. It was one of the most welcomed feelings I have ever had. The crash truck was beside the runway as I exited the plane. It would have been needed if I had run into more problems.

Aircraft carrier showing arresting wires and barriers.

CHAPTER VI

AIRCRAFT CARRIERS AND WHAT WE DO

Carrier landings would be next and our final step before we deployed on the Aircraft Carrier USS Hornet CVA12. It had been some time since any of us made a carrier landing, so a lot of practice was in order. We practiced at an outlying field called Crow's Landing, about a hundred miles south of Alameda. They had a carrier deck painted on the runway, complete with an LSO (Landing Signal Officers) platform. Our LSO was Lt. Ernie Huber. We would take Ernie to sea with us on the Hornet since we would both be familiar with each other and our own little quirks. I think he was among the best in the business.

When we were ready, we would fly out to a carrier in this area and qualify. It was required that Ernie had to give you his OK before you were considered qualified. None of the new pilots had landed a jet on a carrier, so it was a whole new learning experience. We had landed the old prop fighter, F6F Hellcat, on the USS Monterey just before we received our wings, but this would be a new ball game. We landed on the carrier in the Hellcat at about 100 miles per hour, less the carrier's speed. The Cougar would be at about 140 miles per hour, less the carrier's speed. Believe me, things happen fast at 140 miles per hour.

The actual landing would start with a formation of planes approaching the carrier in formation in an upwind direction. As they near the carrier, they will go into a right echelon. In an echelon, each plane is on the same side of the leader in a stair-step position. This is done while approaching the carrier. As the formation passes over and past the carrier, the leader will make a break to the left and each of the remaining planes will follow at regular intervals.

As soon as the break is performed, the pilot will close the throttle and start a descending turn. When the plane gets down to the proper airspeed, the pilot will lower the landing gear by placing the landing gear handle in the down position. When he closes the throttle, a horn will start. This tells him his landing gear are not yet down and locked into position. He will continue to descend in his turn, heading for a position that is going in the opposite direction the carrier is heading and maintaining a wingtip distance from the carrier. A wingtip distance is defined as having his wingtip on the carrier. This will give him the proper distance to make his landing approach.

When the landing gear has come down and locked into position, the horn will stop. There are also indicators telling him each one of the landing gear has locked into position. At this point, he has added power to maintain the proper speed and altitude.

As he continues in a downwind direction and the airspeed reaches a set point, the pilot will lower the flaps and tailhook. Flaps are located in both wings that, when lowered, will allow the plane to fly at a slower speed. When the flaps come down, the forward part of each wing will slide out and slightly down. These are called slats. This will leave an opening between the rear of the slat and the now front edge of the wing. This causes the wind passing through this opening and over the wings to have a smoother airflow. Most people think it is the wind under the wings that keeps the plane in the air when it is actually the wind over the top of the wings. This is what creates lift. If that lift is not smooth it will be lost, and the airplane will stall. A stall is when there is not enough lift on the wings to hold the airplane in flight.

There is one more factor that must be considered. Sometimes that flow of air over the wings is not smooth and in a straight direction. Therefore, some airplanes have a series of short vertical pieces of metal called vanes on the wing to control the flow of air, usually near the fuselage. These vanes will keep that movement of air straight. These are called vortex generators.

The pilot has allowed the airplane to descend and has maintained his wingtip distance from the carrier. He will hold that until he reaches the island of the ship. At this point, he will reduce his power and speed and start a descending turn toward the ship. He will maintain the descending turn and line up with the back, or fantail, of the ship. By this time, the LSO (Landing Signal Officer) has picked him up and will be the controller until he gives him the cut to land or wave-off to go around again.

The LSO has signals he can convey to the pilot with the hand paddles he is holding. Each movement of those hand paddles is telling the pilot what the LSO wants him to do.

If the pilot receives the cut signal, he will immediately close his throttle and direct his eyes away from the LSO and onto the deck of the carrier. He must now flare out enough to make a smooth landing and pick up one of the wires on the deck of the carrier. If he misses a wire or catches a late wire, he may engage the Davis Barriers. These are wire barriers about three feet high that the nose wheel will engage first. As the top wire of the Davis Barrier is engaged with the nose wheel, it will cause a lower wire to come up and engage the main gear. If he missed the Davis Barriers or takes them out, he will end up in the Palisade, which is twelve feet high with vertical nylon straps. These will catch the airplane and hopefully stop it. These straps are so strong, I have seen them snatch an airplane out of the air while it was still flying and stop it. If the landing is uneventful, the pilot will direct his attention to a deck handler. The deck handler will direct him out of the way so the barriers can be raised, and the deck readied for the next airplane.

As the airplane is directed forward, the pilot will fold his wings. The deck handler will take him forward and park him on the forward part of the deck or take him to the hangar deck by way of an elevator.

The take-off from the carrier has been covered earlier in this book. I will review it briefly at this time. The take-off in a Hellcat could be done with a deck roll with no catapult necessary. In a Cougar, it was necessary to be catapulted to get into the air. That meant being accelerated over 100 miles per hour in 200 feet and about two to three seconds.

Once the catapult is fired, the pilot cannot move until he is leaving the ship. When the pilot is hooked up on the catapult and ready to go, he will go to full throttle at a signal from the catapult officer, which is an upheld arm with his hand moving in a circular motion. He then pulls a rod up in front of the throttle and grips both together, so he does not pull the throttle back during the sudden acceleration. He will put his elbow in his stomach and open hand behind the stick after saluting the Catapult Officer letting him know he is ready. He then puts his head back firmly on the headrest and waits. When the Catapult Officer drops his hand and points to the front of the ship, he is on his way and in a hurry.

We had a lot of practice ahead of us. We would practice until we did it right and not just once, but every time. Then we would practice some more. Everyone had a lot of respect for our LSO Ernie Huber. We knew he had our lives in his hands every time we landed on the carrier. Some of those landings were made under challenging conditions. Sometimes there were not a lot of choices about whether you had to fly, but a landing was always mandatory. Landing on a pitching deck can be challenging. I think there is little doubt that landings on a pitching deck were the most challenging landings I have ever made. When the deck is pitching badly, the LSO has a man behind him telling him if the deck was coming up or going down. The LSO must give him the cut at exactly the right time. The pilot could slam into the deck if it is coming up when he makes contact, or if the deck is falling away, he could miss all the wires and end up crashing into the barriers. Needless to say, the LSO is a very important man with a very important job.

For the time being, we just kept our present routine until all preparations were finished to start practicing for the carrier qualifications.

One of my pastimes was to flight test a plane that had just been repaired. It was a requirement that someone had to check it out. I liked this since I could go out for an hour or two and do anything I wanted to do. There just happened to be such an airplane at this time, so I volunteered. After making sure the plane was operating as it should and the problem was remedied, I decided to see how high I could get it, so I just started climbing. Normally we did not get above 40,000 feet because anything above that was very hard to attain. I passed through 40,000 feet and continued climbing, but at a very slow rate. It took a long time to go through 45,000 feet. I finally reached 47,000 feet, but I knew that I was near the top, so I just pulled the stick back, converting what speed I had left into altitude, and gained 300 feet. The airplane stalled and just dropped its nose. I sat there and marveled at the view; I could see the curvature of the earth.

Having time and fuel left, I just rolled over into a dive and made a rapid descent. I could see a mountain range to the west, so I knew I was in Nevada, where the ground was flat and green. This was tempting me to see how fast I could go when flying straight and level. At a low level, if you pass over a dark spot on the ground, such as a plowed field, you may encounter heat thermals. The dark spots absorb heat faster and send it off as rising turbulence. At high speed, they can be deadly to the point of even separating the wings from the rest of the airplane.

I continued down to 2,000 feet and opened the throttle. I watched the airspeed needle climb to 525 knots and was still going. Converted to miles, this would be about 600 miles per hour. The speed of sound is approximately 750 miles per hour. I reduced the throttle, not wanting to push my luck.

Everything was now just routine. We had all the planes back from Fallon, and they were getting a good going-over by maintenance. Jack Snyder had flown the plane back that had landed wheels up, but he had to leave the gear down on the way back. Our Air Group Commander, on take-off from Fallon, had gone through the tops of the trees at the end of the runway. He was very lucky to make it through the trees. However, the plane received damage.

The day finally arrived to start carrier landing practice, which we would work in shifts. Several pilots would fly down to Crow's Landing and practice carrier approaches and landings. After finishing our practice, we would land and refuel before returning to Alameda. The next shift would then take over.

I was in the last shift this particular day. After the practice, I landed and went in to refuel. After refueling, I taxied out to the duty runway. It was customary to perform a standard check-off list before taking off. One of the checks was to test the lateral controls to make sure the emergency flaperettes would cut in if we lost our larger flaperons. Each time I performed the test, the flaperons in both wings stood straight up. If this happened in flight, you would lose complete control of the airplane. There was no question of this. I taxied back to the hanger and asked maintenance to check it out, but there was no one there who knew how to work on them.

I climbed back into the airplane and taxied out to the duty runway again. Checking the flaperons provided the same results. I just sat there and thought for a minute. Crows Landing was in the middle of nowhere and about a hundred miles from Alameda. I would either have to stay the night or face a long ride back by vehicle. I may have been able to put up with that, but I had a date that night with a young lady who had been eluding me. That was the deciding factor.

I pulled onto the runway, again checking my controls. The flaperons again appeared to work OK until they called for emergency control, and then both would stand straight up. I took a deep breath and advanced the throttle to full throttle. I got into the air and avoided as much lateral (side to side) movement as I could. When I could see Alameda, I called the tower, declared an emergency, and requested a straight-in approach. I was given clearance, so I pointed my nose at the duty runway and started to let down. I avoided sideways movement of the stick and tried to use the rudder to steer as much as I could. When I hit the runway, I started to breathe normally again.

The day finally came for us to make our qualifying landings on a carrier. The USS Philippine Sea had been called in just off the coast of California for us to use. The Skipper led the first flight with Sam as number two. Jack Snyder led the second flight with me as number two. We would not wait for the first flight to finish and would all be qualifying together. Everything went well. I had no wave-offs, so I was the first pilot to qualify. Later the Skipper told me, jokingly I hope, that he wanted to be the first to qualify. I was wondering if maybe I should have caused one wave-off and been satisfied with second place.

All our pilots qualified without mishap. Everyone was happy to accept this.

Our LSO Ernie Huber.

CHAPTER VII

GOING TO SEA

We had to go to Norfolk, Virginia, to join our ship. Some flew our planes out while some drove. I drove my car home to Iowa to visit my family. On my drive home, I was having a lot of problems with my left eye. It was very sensitive to light, especially at night when meeting other cars. I finally put some cloth over my eye to shield it from the car lights. It was two thousand miles from Alameda to my home. I drove this with only short stops to nap a little. It was a very stressful drive.

When I arrived home, I made an appointment with Dr. Phelps, an eye doctor that my sister was a nurse for. He discovered that I had developed an ulcer on my left eye. Dr. Phelps was able to remove the ulcer after making several attempts. I had to keep both eyes covered for almost the entire time I was home, which was for about a week. It was not a very enjoyable time while I was home.

My parents drove me to Virginia where my ship the USS Hornet was docked. We were to make a world cruise, encircling the globe and returning to California.

It was undoubtedly to be an experience of a lifetime. We first sailed to Portugal and enjoyed the culture and people of that nation.

We then traveled south and entered the Mediterranean Sea, stopping in Naples, Italy. We visited historic sites and even traveled to Rome. From there, we passed through the Suez Canal into the Indian ocean, stopping at Ceylon. We did have carrier operations, however; I was not able to fly until we entered the Mediterranean Sea because my vision had not yet gotten back to normal. I was back on the flight schedule and eager to join the other pilots in flight operations.

Something just wasn't right with my eyes. I didn't realize it until I started to fly again. I was having a problem landing on the carrier. I never before had a problem landing on a carrier, but suddenly I was. In basic, I never had a wave-off. I made six landings in six passes. In advance, I also never had a wave-off. I had eight landings for eight passes. I was the first man to qualify on the carrier when our squadron had carrier qualifications back in Alameda. I don't recall any wave-offs at that time. I don't think I had ever had a pilot-caused wave off on an aircraft carrier. Now, suddenly I was having trouble. I took seven passes to get aboard on one occasion. It seemed that I was getting high in the final approach as I was landing. After I got aboard, I went to our ready room and shook so badly I couldn't light my cigarette. I kept dropping my lighter. I was just about a basket case.

The Skipper knew something was wrong and sent me to the flight surgeon to have him check my eyes. My eyesight was good, but something had changed. I believe that something was my depth perception. The flight surgeon had not checked my depth perception when he examined me, so it did not surface at that time. I am sure I was seeing things differently than I had before. The procedure to remove the ulcer had been rather extensive and invasive. It had definitely affected my eyesight. I had to learn all over again to adjust for this change in depth perception. It came around rather quickly, and I was back to my old self in a short time.

After leaving Italy, we proceeded to the Suez Canal and made our way slowly down its narrow banks. This was one of the highlights of our journey. We would pass by towns and small settlements as well as military installations such as an Egyptian army camp. At one point we found ourselves in a rather large lake midway through the canal. Ships were stopped here waiting for their turn to continue their journey. Our Carrier was so large that it often filled the canal, so we traveled close to each side. Most of the sides were concrete, making it even more perilous.

We traveled at a very slow speed, proceeding with caution. A wind could affect us very easily and cause us to drift, making navigation difficult. To overcome this, we had our AD dive bombers lined up sideways on the side of the deck. If we started to drift more than we should, the planes would be started and could pull the carrier away from the side of the canal by revving up the engines. This did consume a lot of time to complete our journey through the canal.

After leaving the Suez Canal, we entered the Red Sea, which connected to the Indian Ocean. Our next stop would be Ceylon. Ceylon is inhabited by people of the Indian culture. Rather short of stature and dark-skinned. It is located right off the coast of India.

Ceylon was known for its precious stones that were offered to us everywhere we went. The last night we were there, I was on the dock waiting to return to our carrier when a vendor approached me with three opals. He had named his price, which I did not have. I took out all my remaining Ceylonese money and told him this was what I had, and if he wanted it, he could have it for the opals. It took him a while to make up his mind, but he accepted it. When I was back at the ship, I went to the Officers Wardroom for some coffee. Jim Hargrove was there, so I showed him the stones. He told me they looked fake to him, so he took out his jackknife, laid one of the stones on the table, and hit it just as hard as he could with the knife while holding it by the open blade. It never fazed it one bit.

As you may imagine, the culture was the same as it was in India. They practiced the Buddhist religion. Elephants were used extensively and could be found everywhere. While in these different countries, we found it interesting to explore and see what life was like in unfamiliar places.

On one occasion while in Ceylon, we had a ship's inspection dressed in our white uniforms on board the Hornet. After the inspection, we did a little site seeing. We waved down a taxi and asked to see some of the sites. Our driver informed us that there was a Buddhist parade taking place not too far away. This sounded interesting, so we decided to see what a Buddhist parade was like. It was further than expected, but we found the event and disembarked from the taxi.

We found the people of Ceylon to be about a head shorter than we were, making us stand out in our dress white uniforms. The crowd was enormous; the parade was colorful, and it contained many elephants. Needless to say, we were quite conspicuous and stood out like a sore thumb.

After a while, since we were the only white people within miles, we decided it would be best if we continued our sightseeing somewhere else. Evidently, the folks in Ceylon do not travel by taxi to any extent. Therefore, we found it almost impossible to find a taxi to continue our adventure. We did, however, finally locate one and left rather hastily.

While in Ceylon, the Air Group Commander accompanied several of us when we went ashore on one occasion. We had pooled our Ceylonese money and had just one of their paper bills left. As we were waiting for a boat back to the ship, the Commander tore the bill into pieces and gave us each one piece.

After leaving Ceylon, we sailed south, stopping at Singapore. Singapore had a certain allure for me. Perhaps it was the movies that had portrayed it as an evil place. A place filled with people of questionable virtues. Like pirates or rugged seagoing men.

Perhaps I didn't go to the right places, but I never saw any such people while we were there.

After leaving Singapore, we continued our journey. This continuation allowed us to cross the Equator. We had a huge ceremony at that crossing. It took us from being a Pollywog to being a Shellback. The ceremony was very elaborate, with the shellbacks in charge of the initiation. It was actually rather rough.

All the old Shellbacks organized an initiation for the unsuspecting Polliwogs. We were presented with the Royal Family. It included Neptune himself and even a royal baby.

The Shellbacks found great pleasure in making us crawl through garbage, putting us in stockades to cut our hair off, and urging us along with their shillelaghs. Now this shillelagh was not something to take lightly. It was a hawser (Navy name for a rope) wrapped in tape. Yes, it did sting a bit. All in all, it was a fun time, and all the Polliwogs survived to become Shellbacks.

From there, we sailed toward the Philippines, which would be our main base while in the area. While we were away from the Philippines, the Skipper decided to send me ahead so I could get some more flight time in while the ship was in route. A plane was readied for me so I could fly in ahead of the ship. I had taxied up to the catapults and was hooked up for a launch. The carrier had turned into the wind and increased its speed. I looked down at my instruments as I was getting ready to be launched and noticed my gyro horizon was not looking right. The gyro must have tumbled and was not operating as it should. We had a low overcast that day and I would have been on instruments shortly after I left the ship. This, of course, would not be good. Without the gyro horizon,

I would have had to go to very basic instruments to fly. This is extremely difficult to do, so I had to abort my launch.

The Skipper still wanted me to go into Manila ahead of the carrier, so the captain of the carrier had a destroyer come alongside. A Bosons chair was rigged between the carrier and the destroyer. That is, they rigged lines between the carrier and the destroyer with a chair on one of the lines that one person could sit on. It was then pulled from the carrier to the destroyer by hand with me in it.

That was a thrill I do not care to repeat. The two ships are about twenty or twenty-five feet apart. You are over open ocean while the transfer is taking place. If the ships are rolling at all, you are constantly going up and down with some of the downs quite close to the water. When I left the carrier, it was steady in the water. The destroyer was a different story. The bow was going up and down with it, sometimes plunging deep into the waves. This could send seawater spraying in all directions, including coming over the bow. If I were ever to get seasick, it would be now. Otherwise, the trip to Manilla was uneventful, and I kept everything down. The carrier did not arrive in Manila for a while, so I had free time with nothing to fly.

There just happened to be a P5M squadron located in Manila. The P5M is a very large flying boat and used for patrols. I was extended the offer to ride along on one of these patrols. We would take off in the evening and come back in the morning. We were in the air for about eleven and a half hours.

To start with, we made a jato takeoff. We had big jato bottles on either side of the fuselage which were fired during our takeoff run in the bay and dropped after we were in the air. when they were fired, it gave the plane a tremendous surge of power which propelled it into the air.

After takeoff, all the running lights were turned off and blackout curtains were placed over the windows. I began to wonder where we were going. I found out later that we were going to fly between China and Formosa.

I was curious why we were trying to go undetected. I was starting to get a little tired, so I found a bunk and decided to take a nap. Sometime later someone shook me to wake me up and asked if I knew what the Pescadores Islands looked like. It was then that I found I was riding with a squadron that had just replaced an older squadron in Manila. It was obvious they were lost and thought I was a member of the old squadron that was riding along to help guide them. This was a bit disturbing to me. There wasn't anything I could do, so I laid back down to try to nap some more.

As I lay there, I thought I could hear the engines change pitch, which meant they were changing power settings. Suddenly I felt the plane vibrate as though it had touched down in the water. A little later I thought I could hear the engines change power again, which I interpreted as a takeoff.

I decided to go forward to the cockpit and find out what was going on. When I confronted the pilots, they told me they had done nothing. I guess my imagination had just run away with me, although I have never been fully convinced.

I was asked if I would like to take the first pilot's seat, which I accepted. I sat down and was expecting to be allowed to take control of this beast. I noticed the copilot was sitting with his feet on the instrument panel. No one was flying, it was on autopilot. I just sat there. The radio crackled a bit and informed the copilot to make a heading change. He leisurely put his feet down, reached over, turned an instrument knob a little, and placed his feet back on the instrument panel. I guess I flew a P5M seaplane that night. At least I sat in the first pilot's seat.

When we arrived back in Manila, it was light. We made an uneventful landing and called it a day, or in this case, we called it a night. It was an interesting experience, and one I shall remember.

We made several trips to Japan and Hong Kong. Some of us pilots were even flown to Korea and given a tour of the entire country. We stopped at several airfields and other military bases in Korea. We also visited the front lines next to the demilitarized zone. I believe they wanted us to become familiar with Korea if that conflict should ignite again. There was considerable damage still visible from the war. The trenches were still in place along with the bunkers. We were even taken to where we could see the Freedom Bridge. This is the bridge where the exchange of prisoners took place. It was in a demilitarized zone so we could not visit it but could observe it from a distance.

We worked with an Air Force fighter squadron in Atsugewi, Japan, while we were in Japan. We were the Red Lightning Squadron while they were the Red Devil Squadron. Their commanding officer welcomed us with a little speech when we first arrived. One of his comments was that, in Japan, you could not afford not to be an alcoholic because the whiskey was so cheap. It was only $1.75 a fifth. They then proceeded to show us exactly what he meant. While there, each one of us Navy pilots bunked with an Air Force pilot. We could not enjoy the luxury of whiskey at sea since we were not allowed to have liquor on board the ship. We stood alerts with them. One of my friends told me an alert came in while he was on standby. It was presented this way: "Pilots! mount your birds, tee off, suck up your rollers, and bounce someone." This told them they had an unidentified plane to intercept.

Some of us pilots stayed at the Air Force base to fly our planes back to the carrier when it went back out to sea. There had been heavy winds, so they had not been able to get the carrier away from the dock. Each day we would check to see if they had gotten the ship away from the dock and what the forecast was. If it were for more windy weather, we would do a little partying.

One day, winds were still in the forecast, so we ventured out again that day and evening. The next morning, we received a call telling us they had been able to get the ship out to sea, and we were to fly our planes out to it. None of us were in the best of shape, but we had to go. When we got out to the ship, the sea was anything but calm. I think that had to be one of the more difficult landings I have ever made on an aircraft carrier. We then proceeded with the task force.

The trip to Hong Kong was also very interesting. It is an old city, and the allure was just as present to me as it was in Singapore.

While in Hong Kong, I pulled Shore Patrol duty. I was given the assignment as the officer in charge of that particular unit, which consisted of me and two sailors. We did not encounter any disturbances; however, it was evident how much authority the Shore Patrol had and how much it was respected by the local proprietors. If we went into an establishment, we were usually met by a representative of that establishment. They wanted our approval of how they were doing because I had the authority to shut the establishment down if I saw the need.

Our sailors also were aware that I could cancel their liberty ashore if I felt that was needed. This was not the case this time, we did not encounter any of these situations on this patrol.

We often served as Boat Officer on liberty boats when we were in port and sailors were given liberty to go ashore. This consisted of being in charge of a liberty boat that transported men on shore liberty back and forth to the different ships of our task group. This could be a small craft that held a few men or a landing ship that could carry fifty or more.

If we had all our carriers in port, the number on shore liberty could be substantial. As you may assume, a sailor on liberty is going to have a good time. This good time often included visiting the drinking establishments. When a sailor had been at sea for a long time, some were eager and anxious to consume as much liquor as possible.

As you know, the consumption of liquor often leaves one incoherent and confused. This confusion often extended to the fact that one cannot remember the ship he is on. To prevent this, one ship may require their liberty goers to wear black socks. Another may wear white socks, and still another one white and one black sock.

While Boat Officer, it was not uncommon to see the need to lower a cargo net and place some men in it to haul them aboard. That may sound like an exaggeration, but it is entirely true.

I was the Boat Officer on an LST on one occasion. This stands for Landing Ship Tank. It is just what the name implies. It is capable of carrying large equipment and a large number of personnel to the beach. The entire front drops down so the personnel or equipment can be offloaded quickly and efficiently.

While used as a liberty ship, it would be brought to shore and the front lowered to accommodate the liberty goers. This meant you had a large number of people on board with a vast number being inebriated. When this was the occasion, I had a Marine shore patrol person with me. We would stand in the front as our personnel was loaded. After loading, I would retire to the bridge, which was elevated. I have had a beer bottle thrown at me and splinter on the steel close to me. It is impossible with fifty or more personnel on board to identify the man who threw the bottle. If this happened while in route to the ship. I could stop the boat and start back to shore. I found that when you have a large number of inebriated sailors, they want to go home. I never found the man who threw the bottle, but I know he was subdued by his friends, so I would turn back toward the ships at anchor.

On one of these occasions, while the personnel was boarding. I was in my place at the entrance to the ship when a very inebriated sailor approached me and started to tell me he had just gotten a Dear John letter from his girlfriend. A letter like that is a rejection, and it is impossible to talk to an individual at a time like this, so I just told him to get aboard. He evidently decided life wasn't worth living and decided to end his life by jumping off the ship's rear. We had the screws turning in the rear to hold us in place on the shore. He was dangerously near them. To top it off, a friend jumped in to save him. It was a tense moment, but we retrieved both from the water.

After retrieving him, he sat on the deck of the LST struggling to get up. He evidently wanted to finish what he had started. At this point, he was becoming uncontrollable. As I mentioned, I had a Marine MP with me. I only had to tell the MP that if he got up to hit him. Of course, the man in question heard me say this. It was surprising how he changed. He sat right down. Maybe it was the figure of the Marine MP with a nightstick looming over him.

Telling the Marine to hit him was not what I wanted, and I am sure the Marine was aware of that as well. I just had to do something to shock the man in question and get his attention. I had some fifty or more other men aboard, with many in the same condition he was. I did not care for this duty.

Sam Hubbard.

Wayne Fox.

CHAPTER VIII

BACK TO THE FUTURE

My thoughts of the past faded as I returned to where we were now, near China, headed for Hainan. I had not gotten any rest, as I had hoped to do. I walked out to where Sam was writing his letter when the loudspeaker barked the command for all pilots to report to their ready room. Sam stopped writing and joined me on the way to the ready room.

Most of the pilots were there when we arrived, so we just took our seats and waited. In a few minutes, when all the pilots were present, the Skipper began with, "We have received our orders. When we get a couple of hundred miles out, the Boxer will launch eight planes. Four AD (prop-driven dive bombers) and four Panthers F9F-5 (jet fighter-bombers). They will sweep the area just offshore, where we think the airliner crashed into the ocean. One hundred miles out, we will launch our F9F-6 Cougars (jet fighters) from our carrier to provide further support."

He named the eight pilots that would be in that group. Neither Sam nor I were in it.

"Depending on what they run into will determine what we do next," the Skipper continued. "Try to stay in or near the ready room in case we need to get more planes into the air. We will have four more planes on standby when we get the first reports. We will have more information for you by then, so just sit tight."

There was a bit of shuffling in the back of the room; then, a Lieutenant Commander walked up to the front.

"Gentlemen," he began, "if we make contact with the enemy, someone may go down or go down for any other reason. We do expect hostile people in the area, we want you to be prepared. If you can, locate people dressed mostly in brown. We think they will be the most willing to help. You will each have an American cloth flag to carry. Also, please wear your .38 revolvers. Any questions?"

No one asked any questions, so the Skipper added, "That's all for now. They should be launching off the Boxer soon. Like I said, everyone, stay in or near the ready room. Those of you who will fly in this first round stay here or stay close. Anyone have any questions?" None were asked, so the Skipper just said, "That's all."

It must have been an hour or more that we endured silence, other than the quiet conversations between the pilots in the ready room. The phone rang at the duty officer's desk. The duty officer answered quickly, then listened in silence for several minutes. He hung up the phone, turning to us, saying, "The ADs off the Boxer shot down two Russian

Yak prop fighters. Not much information on it. They had come up to challenge us, and the ADs shot them down. No damage was reported to any of our planes. That's all I was told."

Everyone sat around trying to guess what happened; this went on for about an hour before the Skipper walked back in. Someone called attention as he walked to the front of the room. He began, "The two Yaks were not part of any larger force; they just happened to be in the wrong place at the wrong time. Nothing else was encountered, so our flight has been canceled. We will launch aircraft from all the carriers in the morning and check the entire area. We will set up a CAP (Combat Air Patrol) and intercept anything that comes into our screening area, anything, including airliners. We will post the schedule a little later. That is all the information I have right now. Get some rest; we will be starting early." With that, he left the room.

Sam was near me, so I just asked if he would care to get a cup of coffee. He answered in the affirmative, so we headed for the Officers Wardroom. Many of the other pilots were there, so a good round of discussion followed. We checked the schedule later before we went to dinner and noticed we were both on the schedule. Sam at 0700 hours and me at 0900 hours. After dinner, we just relaxed for the evening before going to bed.

The next few days proved to be rather interesting. We flew a lot, intercepting anything that came close to the task group. I was only on one airliner intercept.

We had been vectored out to intercept an unidentified plane on the radar; when we sighted the plane, we saw that it was an airliner several thousand feet below us. Jack told Bear to stay at their altitude to cover us as we went down to check it out. We came up on the right side of the airliner. Jack held his position while I slipped under it and came up just behind the left wing and moved in very close until I could see the people glued to the windows. I am sure there were some anxious moments inside the airliner. We then left it.

Another time while on CAP, we received a call from the ship that a bogie (unidentified aircraft) was approaching the task group. We were vectored out for an intercept. The CIC (Combat Information Center) kept telling us that the bogie was low on the water and heading directly toward our task group. We dropped down to about 10,000 feet before we picked it up. Jack called the ship and said, "joy," which was the way we told the ship we had it in sight. The ship immediately came back with, "Roger, that's your bogie; take him." They were telling us to shoot him down.

Jack immediately came up on the radio. "Bear, you two stay up here and cover us. Foxy, arm your guns." With that, I simply hit two levers that pumped 20 MM shells into all four cannons. We split off from Bear and his wingman and rolled into a descending turn toward our bogie. Jack was executing a textbook run. We were too far out to get a positive identification on our bogie, but we were closing in fast. We were traveling at about 500 knots, which is approaching 600 miles per hour. We would only have about two to three seconds to fire at that speed. We would only have a few seconds before that time to make a positive identification. I was flying a loose combat formation on Jack, but I was able to notice that my gun site was slightly below the bogie's right wing. That told me that Jack had his sight on the pilot. That is the ideal place to hit the bogie: the pilot is the most venereal part of the airplane. If you can take the pilot out, it's all over.

I slipped out a little more from Jack. I knew I would have to raise my nose a bit to hit the right wing. I just needed a little more room to maneuver. I still had the tip of the bogie's right wing in my sights. I would have to touch the left rudder just a bit to go into a slight skid. This would bring my guns to bear on the inner right wing or pilot if I could get enough of a skid. At six hundred miles per hour, it would be just a touch of the left rudder, nothing more.

The ship called. "Identify him first." They wanted us to be sure it was an enemy before we shot him down. When Jack made the reversal to line up on him, we both realized it was one of our dive bombers. Jack did not have time to tell me, but I noticed it at the same time he did. We would have fired in a few seconds. We passed under him at a very high rate of speed. He never saw us until we were past him. He jerked his plane into a right turn, but it would have been too late.

The AD dive bomber had lost his radio and could not call the ship. In a case like this, he should have performed a designated maneuver so the ship would know he was friendly. It would be a simple maneuver, like flying a circle to the left and one to the right. This was changed often so an enemy would not know what the maneuver would be on any particular day. He was a very lucky man that day.

Jack was hungry for combat. During one of our preflight briefings, he told us that his radio would go out, and we would head to China. His comment was, "We'll get those Migs up." The Mig was a jet fighter made in Russia. We were often just off the coast of China, which had these Mig airplanes.

Bear just said, "Jack, I will follow you anywhere, but when they get me on that long green carpet, I will tell them exactly what happened." I agreed with Bear. That is the way wars are started or pilots lose their lives. I think every pilot secretly wants to test his metal in combat, but pilots do die in combat. Combat is not a game, it's the real deal.

I recall an incident a short time later. We were on Combat Air Patrol when we got a call that four unidentified planes were in our air space, so we were vectored out to intercept them. We did not know who they were, we were just told that they were higher than we were. This put us at a disadvantage. We were near 40,000 feet and they were higher. The Russian Mig could fly higher than we could, so this was an indication that it could be Migs. The sun reflected off of them, which made them appear to be silver; we were in blue. I was convinced they were Migs. We started to gain altitude and maneuvered for position, hoping they had not seen us. As we did, my heart was pounding so hard, I was sure it was making my lifejacket jump. I was sure this was going to be my baptism of fire. It turned out that it was four of our planes off a sister carrier. I am not sure if I was relieved or disappointed.

The incident with Bear and Jack earlier about going into Chinese airspace dampened the idea Jack had to get some Migs up in China. That is until Jack and I were out alone. We were off the coast of China, which we could plainly see. He pointed to his earphones and gave me a thumbs down, which was telling me that his radio was out. He then, with his hand, pointed towards China. There was little doubt about what he was telling me. We were heading for China to get some Migs up. I saw no need to start a war or get killed, so I just came up on my radio and asked him what he said. That way, the ship knew my radio was working.

We did have our opportunity later to enter Chinese airspace. Our flight was on the schedule to fly, so I went to the ready room for our preflight briefing. When I arrived, I was greeted by Marine guards on both doors. No one was allowed in the ready room except the pilots who would fly the mission, a briefing officer, and the duty officer.

The briefing officer began. "Gentleman, this is a secret mission. You will be escorting a photo plane into China. The Admiral wants pictures of the defenses on the outer islands off China in case something should erupt. We are in a tense situation that could turn into something bigger. The Admiral wants to know how well fortified the outer islands are in case this does escalate into something more. You will stay at 40,000 feet to cover the photo plane. We are quite certain that the Chinese will launch Migs. The photo plane will make one run over the islands and head directly for home. You are to keep the Migs off him. If they appear to be going after the photo plane, you are to intercept them. The photo plane will be in and out so fast that the Migs should not be able to intercept him. We think the Chinese are used to us flying near their airspace so they will not launch the Migs right away. If they appear to have a chance to catch the photo plane, you are to prevent that. Otherwise, you are to return immediately. We would like to prevent making contact with the Migs if possible. Your job is to protect the photo plane. Remember, once the photo plane is safe, go home."

On the mission, I could not see the photo plane make his photo run because we were too high. He did receive a lot of ground fire and took one minor hit. We were in and out of China so fast the Migs never got to us. There is little doubt that Migs were launched, we just surprised them and acted too fast for them.

The end results were that no one got hurt, and the Admiral got his pictures. Jack also got his chance to enter Chinese airspace. I had a lot of admiration for Jack. Later Jack had to eject from an F8U fighter at supersonic speed and survived. He also was shot down in Vietnam and had to eject over water. He was an excellent pilot and a very brave man. I was honored to be his wingman.

It was a very tense time for a few days. Several times when they had picked up Russian bombers heading toward us, we would be called to general quarters (battle stations) on the ship and told an attack was imminent. The CAP could not get to them in time to intercept them, so the CAP was told to break right (get out of the way). We are going to salvo (start shooting at them). I have been on the deck in my plane as a backup for a launch when the ship announced that they had picked up airborne Migs.

While we were near Hainan, we often flew CAP. On one occasion there were just two of us. When we were relieved, we went into a near vertical dive at full throttle. When we reached the sound barrier, I could see a thin condensation line form on my partner's wing and my wing as well. It started from the leading edge of the wing and moved back on the wing and went straight out. This was on both sides of the wing, and on both of our planes. The faster we went, the further the vapor wall moved back on the wing. This was the actual sound barrier. I never saw this before and never again. The conditions must have been just right for condensation to form. This was all taking place in 1954. Supersonic flight was new to the fleet. It was a learning experience, and even more so, an adventure.

Cougar on a wave-off.

Cougars unfolding wings, preparing for the catapult.

Cougars on the catapults.

Cougars being launched.

F9F-5 Panther after deck crash.

Cougar in the fence.

Sunken ships in Manila Bay from WWII.

Getting ready.

READY ROOM of the *Hornet's* Squadron 91,
...ar a flyer tell how he met Red planes which
...g tip to wing tip with him, then disappeared.

SUNDAY MUSIC (*Onward, Christian Soldiers*
A Mighty Fortress is Our God) is supplied by
Yorktown's organist ... bar ... deck ...

A picture in Life Magazine. It contained a caption saying that one of our pilots met a red (Russian) airplane and flew wing tip to wing tip with it. Entirely untrue. I am on the far right under the arrow.

Ready room on the hornet. Wayne Fox, second row in the middle. Sam Hubbard back row with a cloth cap.

CHAPTER IX

THINGS HAPPEN

On a rather sad note, one of the Panther pilots had gone over the side of the carrier in his plane and did not survive. I talked to him a few days before when he had shown me a picture of his wife and children. The only thing they were able to recover was a map case with these pictures. What makes it even sadder for his family is that this was the second son they had lost as a Navy pilot. There was a burial at sea ceremony held for him.

Landing accidents are very common on an aircraft carrier, occurring almost every day of flight operations. I was in two of them. One was a minor engagement with the smaller barriers called the Davis Barriers. They can stop a plane with only minor damage to the undercarriage if they are engaged soon enough, but if a plane hits the 12-foot high Palisade, the damage can be much worse.

I had been on patrol and was just returning to the ship. It was late in the day and near dusk. Two of the planes in front of me had gone into the barriers, including the palisade. The last had a major engagement and damaged the barriers and palisade, making it necessary to re-rig them. I went up a little higher so I would burn less fuel while they did the re-rigging, which was taking a rather long time. Long enough for it to get dark. The deck edge lights were lit up, and the LSO would use lighted wands. I came down and made a normal break onto the downwind leg. It was fairly dark by this time. As I turned onto the final approach, I started to get a little high. Being my first night carrier landing, this was all new to me. The LSO waved me off, so I applied full power and pulled up to go around again.

On the next pass, I started to get a little high again. The LSO started to give me another wave off, but he was using a new style of unfamiliar lighted hand wands and had the light cord wrap around a deck edge light. This made it impossible for him to raise that wand for a wave-off. He then gave me the cut signal to land, but this was a late cut, and I was too high. I took out all the barriers I engaged and caught a late deck wire. I entered the larger palisade at a rather high speed, taking that out as well.

Every accident must go by a review board. This board gave me an accommodation for averting a major aircraft accident. Many pilots would have made a dive for the deck, trying to snag a wire. They could easily hit the deck so hard it would cause them to jump over the barrier and into the parked aircraft. It had happened to us recently, causing major damage to several aircraft. Surprisingly, there was only one minor injury in that accident.

I did mention before that the top wire of the palisade can slide up the nose of the airplane and jump into the cockpit. To prevent this, when the tail hook is lowered, a smaller hook pops up just in front of the windshield to catch it. It is worth mentioning again because it was something to be aware of and be prepared for.

The tension in the atmosphere had lessened, so we relaxed a bit and went back to our old routine. One of our pilots, Carlos Baker, had his plane catch fire just after he left the catapult, but it quickly extinguished itself. It left him with damaged controls, making it impossible for him to land on the ship. We were close to Formosa, so it was thought he might be able to make it there to land. He was fighting the control constantly and was unsure if he could make it, so he decided to eject over the ship and have a helicopter pick him up out of the water. Everything went well, and he did eject. On the way down, he was able to make movies with a camera he had with him. Life Magazine paid him to be the first to look at them. However, they had been ruined by the saltwater.

I was not very sure about Life Magazine. Earlier, when they were on our ship near Hainan, Life Magazine had published a picture of a group of us pilots in our ready room and labeled it as pilots listening to another pilot tell how a Russian Airplane had joined up on him and flew wingtip to wingtip. A total fabrication. There would have been bullets flying long before that happened.

We received a notice that said the Air Force F-86 Saber Jet was flaming out when all six of their 50-caliber machine guns were fired at high altitude. I am not sure if they considered me good or expendable, but they sent me to 40,000 feet to fire some long bursts with all four of my 20 mm cannons. Nervously, I did it and was rewarded with the engine unphased.

Our tour on the line was coming to an end, so we stopped in Japan to offload our planes. We then sailed to Hawaii for a short stop before going on to San Francisco and home. We spent a short time in Hawaii, which was interesting. To visit the Battleship Arizona was truly a step back in history that was a reminder of the men who gave their lives in defense of our country. This was only the beginning, and many more men and women would follow.

It becomes more difficult for me, as time goes by, to understand why hostilities continue to take place. The more I witness, the less I understand why people want to kill each other. In the end, it all becomes for naught. After a time, it appears that the world goes back to where it was, and everyone is friends again. I don't know how it can be forgotten and accepted that soon. We should not harbor hatred, I know. The question I have is why it happened in the first place. Maybe the leaders should stand in front of their warriors and lead instead of pushing from the rear. I don't think we would have as many wars if this were the case. I know this is not possible and so do the leaders. Because of this, it will continue.

When we arrived in San Francisco, a large crowd was there to greet us. I picked my parents out of the crowd as we pulled in to dock the Hornet. It was a wonderful reunion and one that can never be forgotten. We had been gone for nine months, had been in many countries, and had circled the globe. It was not only the trip of a lifetime, but also something that few people experience. It was also rare that we were paid to do something like this. It was not without danger, but we did far better than many who have traveled such a road ahead of us.

My parents had driven from Iowa to take me home before I reported to my next duty station.

It was nice to go home again, even if for only a short time. I had not seen many of my old friends for a rather long time. Most of the men that joined the Navy with me were being released from the Navy. I still had active duty time, to which I was obligated.

I think I was looking forward to returning to my duty station. The Navy was now like another family to me. The other men were like my brothers. We were together constantly and learned to depend on each other. That has never changed and never will.

Sam modeling in Ceylon.

Sam in the Philippines.

Royal family while crossing the Equator.

Crossing the Equator, Joe Saline.

In memoriam
omas Moir Gardiner, USN
27 July 1954

Burial at sea for Thomas Gardiner.

CHAPTER X

BACK IN THE STATES

My next duty station was the Training Command in Pensacola, Florida. Sam was assigned there too, so we decided to bunk together again. We had both made Lieutenant junior grade by this time.

After my short leave at home, I had driven to Pensacola where I met Sam. Since we both had a limited time left on our commitment to the Navy, we decided to stay in the BOQ (Bachelor Officers' Quarters) until we had completed our remaining time.

We went through the Instructor Training School and were sent to Whiting Field to instruct students. Sam's home was in Centerville, Alabama, which was not very far away. We often went there on the weekends to visit his family. He had a great family who seemed to accept me even though I was a Yankee. Sam was named after his father, so his name was also Sam, and his mother was Elizabeth. She was so good to me, I almost felt as though she was my mother too. He had a younger sister, Jane, and an even younger brother, Mike. His grandparents, the Moodys, gave me the same Christmas present they gave Sam. I remember Sam remarking that I must be one of the family now. We often visited Uncle Bert and spent time with his cousins, the Parks brothers. Sally Poe was an old friend who we often saw. Sam had a wonderful family, and I grew to love every one of them.

Teaching students was not that bad. It was satisfying to see a young man learn to fly, and even more importantly, learn to fly the Navy way. It had its downside as well, like seeing a student struggling to achieve something he wanted so desperately to do. Of course, there was the inevitable. Accidents and fatalities were always there, and sometimes they raised their ugly heads. Accidents were common, as you might expect, with young men learning to fly. I was told in later years that my first student was killed in an accident. I had worked so hard with him and thought he would be able to finish his training without much difficulty. Sometimes it didn't matter how good you are, it was often down to the luck of the draw.

Besides instructing my own students, I was designated as a check pilot; an instructor who, other than a student's instructor, would ride with the student to determine if he was ready to move on to the next step in his training. It could be a big decision for the check pilot, especially if the student was to start flying solo.

As a check pilot, I would check the student in the early phases of his flying. He would have had previous check flights along the way, but one, in particular, was to let him go up alone for the first time. There would be no one to get him out of trouble. He would have to do it on his own, which could be a huge decision for the check pilot. The decision was made at a large grass practice field. The final step was to go to this designated outer field and have the student make several landings while you are in the plane. If you told him to come to a full stop on the next landing, the student knew you were going to get out and let him go alone. You would have him taxi back to a take-off area, get out and tell him to make a designated number of landings, stop and pick you up. On the way back to the main field, I would tell him if he passed. I knew it would be eating at him. I told one student, if he could land back at the main base and taxi the plane back to the parking area, I would give him an up. He replied that he would get it there if he had to carry it.

The students were usually ready to solo, so it was uncommon to have to give them a down. On one occasion, I had to do this. I think it hurt me as much as it did him. We were shooting landings at a concrete practice field. While doing so, he was coming in a little high, letting the main wheels hit first. It was before we had tricycle gear, so he would then go jack rabbiting down the runway.

We were not supposed to instruct a student on a check flight, but I thought it would help him pass his check if I gave him a small hint. I told him to get the stick back to the full stall position when he was on the runway. A full stall is when you have eliminated all the lift on the wings and the plane can no longer stay in the air. It had to remain on the ground in this condition. These were full stall landings, making it necessary to keep the stick pulled back into your lap at the proper time.

On the next landing, he dropped the plane in from about 25 or 30 feet and jerked the stick all the way back. I rode with my hand behind the stick, but I was unable to stop this sudden movement. The plane reacted by the nose coming up to a near vertical attitude. In this near vertical position, it went into a complete or full stall. I grabbed the stick, slammed it forward, and added full throttle. While doing this I also added full left rudder to try to bring the right wing up, but I was unable to recover before we hit the runway with the right wing and right landing gear. The end of the right wing was bent up considerably, but the landing gear stayed intact. If I had been a second slower, I am sure we would have cartwheeled. It would have been difficult to survive. If the right landing gear had failed, we would have surely contacted the runway with the nose and fuselage in a downward attitude. There would also be a strong chance of a fire when the engine made contact with the runway. All it takes is a ruptured fuel line and a spark.

A friend of mine had his student in a landing pattern at about 500 feet to practice touch and go landings. The student was flying and somehow stalled the airplane, which then flipped inverted. Before my friend could take control, the student had pulled the stick back, putting them into a nose-down vertical position. It was impossible to recover from that attitude. They hit the ground at a rather steep angle.

The student was killed in the front seat. My friend was jammed under the instrument panel when his seatbelt and shoulder straps failed. He had massive injuries. When I saw him last, he was walking, but would never fly again. It would take a massive blow to make your safety belt fail. Later, when I crashed in a jet, I was contacting trees with such force it severed both wings and tail sections. My safety straps held, but I had solid bruises under the straps.

I scrapped another wingtip with a student another time while making crosswind landings. It was considered a minor accident.

My first student was Roy Meadow. Roy was a nice young man with average abilities who had a little difficulty with some maneuvers, which was not unusual. I would often stay out longer to give him extra instructions. I was new at this and still in a learning period myself. Some pilots who start a little slower can end up as one of the better pilots. Roy, however, was not slow by any means. I felt he was doing OK and had passed all his check hops. I was told that after he left our field; he lost his life in a plane accident. I don't know if it was true. I just didn't care to dwell on it further, so I never tried to find out.

Pilots have a superstition that accidents happen in a series of three. I still think that is true.

When the new trainer, the T-34, was introduced, I was selected to be one of the first instructors to fly and instruct in it. It had tricycle landing gear and was a dream to fly. I ended up with over 600 hours of flight time in the T-34. Almost all were instructing either students or new instructors.

Sam and I always had a good time together, whether it was in Pensacola or at his home. We did date a lot, but neither of us wanted to settle down just yet. We spent a lot of time at his home and dated a couple of girls we had met at a nearby college. The girl Sam dated had a father that was worth eight million dollars, so she received the nickname Eight Million. Of course, that was only between Sam and me.

At this time, Miss Universe was going to make an appearance in the Pensacola area. The Navy would be in charge and have her escorted around to different functions. One officer on the committee asked me if I would be her escort. It took me less than two seconds to say yes. Before the event occurred, a married Lieutenant on the committee said he wanted to do it, so that left me out in left field somewhere. Never did like that guy.

The day arrived for both Sam and me to leave the Navy. That was a rather sad day. Sam and I had been friends and lived together for about three years, so we agreed to keep in touch. Sam left a little before me, but I couldn't get over the habit of going to Centerville, Alabama, so that continued until I, too, left the Navy.

Two other friends, George Crain and Bill Shumway, and I had decided to go to college in Colorado after we finished our tour of duty. George had joined the reserves in Chicago and was a weekend warrior. It was an excellent way to get some extra cash if you needed it. George was in a flight of four jets that was entering the landing pattern in a diamond formation. This formation was not normal and considered a little risky on the breakup to enter the downwind leg.

I was told that the pilot behind George broke into him, causing a major collision. George tried to eject, but he was too low and inverted. His chute never deployed. He, of course, did not survive. I did not inquire about the other pilot, as there was little need even to ask. It also terminated our college plans.

George's full name was George Washington Crain III. I am not sure if his lineage included the legendary George Washington. I never thought to ask. George was a very handsome man, looking a lot like Christopher Reeve. His father was a prominent psychiatrist in Chicago. I think George had a lot going for him.

George used to like to go to New Orleans in his free time and asked me to accompany him on one occasion. When we arrived in New Orleans, we checked into a hotel. George was on the phone for some time. When he hung up, he told me we each had two dates that evening. With a surprised look, I asked, "What in the world are we going to do with two dates each?" George looked at me with an inquisitive look and said, "Just pick out the one you like best." I am not sure how George proposed to do that. I don't even recall how he did. I am sure George had a method.

George did have the resemblance of George Washington, so I would not have been surprised if he was related to him.

CHAPTER XI

BACK HOME TO IOWA

I wasn't sure what I wanted to do or where I wanted to go when I was released from the Navy. My home was in Iowa, but I had an uncle and aunt in Florida. I did not have any firm plans, so it was up in the air. I drove to the outskirts of Pensacola and tried to make up my mind. I finally decided to flip a coin to make that decision. It was rather a crude way, but going home to Iowa won.

I was completely lost at home. I was now twenty-five years old and still single. It appeared that everyone I knew was married. No guys to hang out with. Just a bunch of married guys that had a wife to answer to. It didn't take long to grow tired of this.

After I was home for a while, I missed the fun Sam and I had while we were in the Navy. I don't know who called who, but I think I told Sam to pack his bags because we were going somewhere. I didn't know where, but we were going. I don't think Sam hesitated very long with an answer.

I drove to Alabama to pick Sam up. We may have spent time with the Parks brothers. It was hard not to do so. We started for Florida and eventually ended up in Miami Beach. I don't remember how long it took, but we ran out of money on the way. We were staying at a motel, so we asked the motel operator to send a telegram for us. It was to my folks, simple, and to the point. "Car trouble, send money." The motel owner asked us what our car trouble was. Sam told him we got the thing down here and can't get it home. I think he had to turn away laughing.

We received the money. Just enough to get us home and started north. We stayed in Silver Springs the first night. We had just checked into our motel when we noticed two girls checking into the unit next to us. Not wanting to miss such an opportunity, we flipped a coin to see who would go over to meet them. Sam lost. Or won. Depends on how you look at it. He bravely spruced himself up a bit and ventured next door.

He was back in a few minutes. I, eager to know the outcome, pressed him for an answer as to how he did. He told me things went well, and that he had invited them out to dinner. I looked at him with a dazed look on my face. He asked me what was wrong. I said, "Sam, we don't have any money."

"Guess I didn't think about that. We'll just have to see what happens."

We did meet them and ventured out to find a place to eat. Sam, at the appropriate time, summoned up the courage to tell them we were void of funds necessary to pay for the food. I believe I was hiding under the table at the time. Since I did not hear any plates shattering over Sam's head, I must have assumed it was safe to come out. I am not sure if it happened exactly that way, but we escaped with our lives. We may have even gotten a free meal. I don't recall. I had placed my faith in Sam to be able to talk his way out of this situation. I'm not sure how he accomplished the task, but we eluded their anger.

It proved to be a fun trip, even with our lack of money, but we had Sam's ability to get us out of trouble. We made another trip later with the Parks brothers, but I won't even touch on that. Somehow, we all survived.

I decided to attend college after I returned home. At least I would be among younger people. The problem was they were too young. They were students just out of high school starting college. I had been in the Navy for over five years and I was several years older. I managed to get two semesters in out of a three semester year. I was doing alright by maintaining a B average, but it was going to take a long time to find the light at the end of the tunnel.

Sam said he was thinking about studying medicine. I looked into that also, but I had so little college experience that I would be an old man when I finished. I decided to try for a pilot in the airlines, so I contacted several preferred airlines. I did land an interview with United Airlines and was flown into Chicago for an interview. I had thought ahead and obtained my commercial and multi-engine license as well as my instrument rating shortly after leaving the Navy. In Chicago, I learned I would have to start as a flight engineer at $450 a month. I had been making $600 in the Navy with my flight pay.

I then learned Sam was going back in the Navy. I guess I had more fun in the Navy than anywhere else, so I thought maybe I should too. It didn't take me long to make up my mind. I requested the necessary forms for a recall to active duty.

Sam had gone back into the training command, so I considered that was as good a place as any to start. I received my orders back to active duty beginning in November 1957. I was happy with that decision and ready to get started.

I was anxious to get to Pensacola, so I drove straight through without stopping. I was exhausted when I arrived, and in much need of some rest. After checking in, I found my quarters and went to bed. I slept for a very long time.

When I woke up, I found Sam and talked to him. He had been asked to join the instructor's school, which was a very prestigious position reserved for the better pilots. I understood it was a requirement to be rated in the top 10% of the pilots to even be considered to join this organization. Then, you could only join by being requested to do so by the commanding officer of that unit. Sam was flying the T-28. I would be assigned to train in the T-34, so he would not fly with me.

I had to attend ground school first to learn the basics of being an instructor. I had instructed before I left the Navy earlier, so it would not be an entire mystery. After ground school, I moved to the flying part of the school. I was flying the T-34 again and loved it. It was like seeing an old friend.

The flying went well for me. I often received credit for several lessons on one flight. The fact that I had instructed before was of some help. However, flying is an art and based more on ability than anything else. I have always felt at home and comfortable in an airplane.

When I started flying as a cadet, my first instructor accused me of having some experience flying. There is an old saying that an average pilot buckles himself into the airplane, but a good pilot buckles the airplane to him. The airplane becomes a part of you, an extension of your arms and legs.

I was told later by one of the yeomen (book and record keepers) in the instructor's school, that I had the highest flight grade that he had seen go through the school since he had been there.

After finishing the instructor's school, I reported to the training squadron based at Whiting Field. Whiting Field was the first step for all cadets to start their hands-on experience training in an airplane. They would learn the basics and solo for the first time at Whiting. Within a couple of weeks, I heard from Commander McLinn, who was the Commanding Officer of the instructor's school. He extended an invitation to me to come back to NAS Pensacola as a staff instructor and instruct the new instructors. It was something that I considered an honor.

It also meant I would be back in Pensacola, instructing with Sam at the same school. Sam and I rented a house in Pensacola near the base.

Bill Russ, a friend of ours, was also at this school. Sam, Bill, and I had been friends for several years. Bill had even named two of his boys after Sam and me. Bill was married to a lovely girl named Ann. Being married precluded his hanging out with us. We still saw each other a lot and maintained a solid friendship.

Bill had been in the same air group Sam and I was in while we were stationed in California and also onboard the USS Hornet. We were in VF-91 while Bill was in VF-94. We were all on the Hornet for the world cruise In 1954.

While at BSG (Basic Standardization Group), which was the instructor's school official name, Bill had been assigned to work on a new jet trainer that was being introduced into the training command. It was the T2J. I never flew it or assigned to work on it, but I went along with Bill to North American Aviation in St Louis to talk to their representatives and test pilots. Somehow Bill and I got the Skipper to let me go along with him. The Skipper put up a fight, but we finally won.

It was an interesting trip. We saw a lot of what North American Aviation was doing in the way of new aircraft. We were shown a new jet that was capable of delivering a nuclear device out the rear of the plane. I believe this particular aircraft may have been switched to a photo reconnaissance plane. If so, it was later flown by a friend of mine in Vietnam. It could reach the speed of twice that of the speed of sound, which is 1,500 miles per hour. We were also wined and dined in high fashion. The highlight for me was talking to and seeing films the test pilots had made.

As noted earlier, Bill Russ was a very good friend of mine and Sam Hubbard, we were all very close. As mentioned before, Bill was stationed where Sam and I were and served in the same air group. Bill did not share some of Sam's and my adventures because he was married and had another commanding officer restricting him. That commanding officer, again, was named Ann.

I mentioned before that Bill named his first son after himself, the second son after me, and the third son after Sam. I considered that an honor, especially because all were fine men like their father. The son named after Sam became a Naval Aviator like his father and Sam.

Bill left the Navy at about the same time Sam and I did. I found out later he was called back to active duty, I believe during the Vietnam war.

I was never called back to active duty and often wondered why. I am sure now, after giving it more thought, it was because I had requested a recall to active duty about the same time Sam did. Since I had been recalled once, they did not recall me again. I did request to be transferred to the regular Navy in my last active duty period. I was turned down. I had been injured in a plane accident earlier and had been unable to fly for several months. That and a lack of a college degree may have been the reason.

My Commanding Officer, Cmdr. McLinn called me into his office and said he would guarantee my acceptance if I would put in another request for Regular Navy. I declined because I felt the reason that kept me out now, would reappear when I went up for higher ranks.

A couple of weeks later, I was offered the opportunity to try out for the Blue Angels. I declined this offer as well.

After being called back to active duty, Bill transferred to the regular Navy and retired as a Captain. A Captain in the Navy is equivalent to a Colonel in the other branches of the service.

While in the Navy, Bill attended the Navy War College. It was an honor to be selected for the War College, it appeared to be reserved for the men who would later occupy significant command positions. This proved to be true for Bill: he commanded a fighter squadron, VF-216, which was a reserve squadron. He also served on the Aircraft Carrier Essex as one of the ship's officers. He was a senior officer in the ship's flight operations division.

Bill flew the F8U Crusader in his command, the same plane Sam spent a lot of time in. The F8U was called the last of the gunfighters. It had been designed for aerial combat and was the last to fill that role.

Like most Navy Pilots, Bill was not a stranger to the dangers of flying. In his early career, Bill was assigned to a squadron that flew the FJ Fury. The Fury was the Navy version of the Air Force F-86 Saber. It was simply an F-86 converted to configurations for Naval Carrier operations.

The Fury also had a terrible record in the Navy. The engine was unreliable and would often explode while in flight. The explosion was so sudden and violent the pilot often had little or no time to eject. The results were that many pilots were lost. Bill related a story about the time four of their planes went out on a routine flight from their squadron location. Three of the planes exploded in flight, leaving only one to return. The other three pilots did not survive.

After leaving the Navy, Bill flew with the airlines as did his son Sam, who had followed his father's footsteps as a Navy pilot.

At one point, I thought Bill was unhappy with me because we had not been in contact with each other for many years. However, that is a two-edged sword. I also failed to contact him. The friendship that we enjoyed could never be broken. It could endure any test.

It was in Pensacola where I also met Mac McMurtry and Tom Cassidy. all became close friends. Sam and I had moved to a house just outside the main gate on the bay with a dock. Tom and Mac had a house on the bay a little further up with a bigger dock. Their house, logically, became the best place to have parties.

We met a group of schoolteachers and other young ladies that lived near us. We just ended up being good friends and dating a lot. The schoolteachers were fine young ladies with high morals. The kind you would take home to meet Mom and Dad.

There were some others around as well. I remember one night it was rather late when the phone woke me up. It was a girl we had met, but never dated. After I said hello, she said, in a rather inebriated voice, "If you are any kind of man at all, you will be over here in ten minutes."

Sam was in a bedroom a short distance away, so I just yelled at him. "Sam, it's for you."

Sam, still half asleep, said, "OK." He came out and picked up the phone. After a brief pause, I heard, "I'll be right over."

He then proceeded to return to his bed. I couldn't help but ask.

"Was it an important call?"

All I heard back was, "No."

We both went back to sleep. I couldn't help but chuckle a bit.

I met a lovely lady by the name of Kay. She had been married to a Navy pilot who was killed in a plane crash in Italy. She was one of the most attractive girls I have ever met in my life. She always looked like she had just stepped off the cover of a fashion magazine. Kay would truly turn heads and was just as nice as she was pretty. I did take her to see my mom and Dad when they were in Florida on vacation. She had one problem: she wanted to get married again. I just wasn't ready for marriage.

I loved being attached to BSG. It was interesting, and we received perks. A directive came out that any plane being checked out for private use, such as going home for the weekend, must have two pilots in it, except the pilots in BSG, which was us at the instructor's school. I don't believe that was received very well. We also had a great group of pilots. People you liked to call a friend.

FJ Fury Bill flew in VF-94 before the F9F-5 Panther.

Bill Russ in an F8F Bearcat while in training.

Bill (Standing 2nd from right) with friends by F8F.

Bill (far left) on the Hornet in front of an F9F-5 Panther.

CHAPTER XII

THE TT-1 PINTO

If a new training plane was being considered for use in the Training Command, it would be given to BSG to evaluate and write a training program for students to follow. Such was the TT-1 Pinto built by Temco in Texas. There were only about fourteen of these aircraft manufactured. One had been lost by one of their test pilots and one by a Navy test pilot. We received nine. I am not sure what happened to the others. LCDR. Pinkepank, Lt. Burt, and I were assigned to evaluate it and create a training program to be followed. I had advanced to the rank of senior lieutenant by this time. I did not like the airplane. It had many fallacies I felt would be difficult for a student to deal with. It had a very short flight duration and was considerably underpowered. If water puddles were contacted on the runway by the nose wheel, the water would be directed into the jet intakes, and a flameout would follow. One time, I flamed the engine out three times on one landing and had to stand on the brakes to stop. After each flameout, I would restart the engine only to experience another flameout. The longest I ever kept one in the air was 1.1 hours, and I was critical on fuel when I landed.

I flew this airplane 22 times. On the 22nd hop, I was going to fly, and LCDR. Pinkepank was going to take notes on how the airplane reacted to stalls and other such unusual maneuvers. We taxied out to the takeoff runway but experienced a defective fuel control and had to return to the line. A defective fuel control would be evident by not being able to control the flow of fuel to the engine with the throttle located in the cockpit. It was rather late in the day, but we decided to try it again with another airplane. We taxied out to the duty runway for the second time. I did a check of the airplane just short of the runway and called for takeoff clearance. We received clearance, so we taxied onto the runway and into the takeoff position. I advanced the throttle to full throttle, made sure everything was functioning correctly, and released the brakes.

The takeoff roll was normal, and we lifted off normally. At about 100 feet altitude, I raised the wheels. I heard the wheels hit the wells, and the well doors close. Immediately a violent explosion in the engine followed. We found out later that it was a blade separating from the turbine and causing others to fail as well. This engine, a J-69, turned up at 22,000 RPM. The jet fighter's engine that I had flown, a J-48P8 engine, turned up at 11,700 RPM. To me, the J-69 engine was an accident waiting to happen. When our engine failed, all we had around us was a pine forest with a drainage ditch leading to the bay. The drainage ditch had utility poles right down the center of it all the way to the bay. We had no chance to reach the bay, so the utility poles became a factor to consider and ruled the drainage ditch out.

We teach a new pilot never to turn back to the airfield after an engine failure at a low altitude. In a turn, you lose altitude faster and a steep turn stall can easily follow because of the loss of lift on the wings. I had been flying for a long time and had a lot of experience, so I felt I could handle it, or at least make a calculated effort to reach the field. I felt we had no other choice to survive unless we could make it back to the field and avoid the heavy growth of trees and brush, so I stood the plane on the right wing. I kept it there long enough to get the plane turned to more of a direction toward the airfield, but not quite enough.

I saw then I was not going to clear the trees and reach the airfield. I would be about 50 yards short. Suddenly a dirt road popped up almost in my line of flight. It was beside the field cut through the trees between us and the field with about forty or fourth-five yards of small trees and brush between it and the airfield. I felt I had a chance to reach it, and a glimmer of hope once more became reality. I knew it would be close, and we may hit a couple of trees before I could reach the road. Even if I did, I would hit the road at a slight angle. The trees were smaller there and much of the terrane was only brush between it and the field. I was hoping I could keep most of the plane in the open road. However, there was a car on the road, and it was apparent that I would touch down right behind or on top of it. I was sure we would not survive whether I took the trees beside the field or hit the car on the road. Not wanting to take the lives of whoever was in the car,

I just leveled the wings and went into the trees alongside the car and road. I am not sure if I would have made it to the road, but I had a chance. Luck was with me again, I dropped into an area that I had not seen that had fewer, smaller trees. I severed the first trees that were only about five inches thick; I believe I lost a wing there. The next trees were larger, so the airplane just started coming apart. The other wing came off and the nose of the plane was shredded. A tree tore off the tail. When this happened, it jerked the rudder pedals back violently. The rudder cables were stressed and failed. I had my feet on the rudders, so they were jerked back violently before the cables snapped.

I was sure my back was broken as that happened, but I was also convinced we would not survive. I can still see the brown, green, and yellow colors going by the canopy as we plowed through the trees and brush. When the plane came to a stop, I was not sure if I was alive or dead. I figured if I were dead, I wouldn't be hurting so much.

The scissor canopy came up a few inches and stopped. The brush on top of it was too heavy to let it open any further. I released my shoulder harness and seat belt. The radio cord and oxygen mask hose separated as I started to get out. I was able to slide over the side and down to the ground, unable to move because of the pain in my back. I heard Pinkepank shouting that he could not get the canopy open enough for him to exit. I managed to stand up and lift the canopy enough for him to slide out to the ground. I am not sure how I accomplished this as heavy as it was with all the brush on top of it. I noticed there was smoke coming from the engine, so we had to get away in case a fire erupted or it exploded.

When the wings came off, the fuel cells in the wings were ruptured. The entire area around the plane was drenched in jet fuel. I somehow made it part way up the trail we had cut through the brush when we crashed. I am not sure how I managed to get past the no longer attached tail section that was in my path. That was as far as I could go. I simply was unable to move, so Pinkepank dragged me further away from the plane.

Jets usually blow up or burn in a crash like this one, but for some reason, this one did not. I think the fire had been extinguished in the engine when it failed in the air, but all that was needed was one spark to ignite the hundreds of gallons of jet fuel that had been spilled. With all the metal coming apart, I am not sure how this was avoided. There was visible smoke coming from the plane when we exited, but still no fire The crash truck crashed through the chain-link fence that encircled the field as well as small trees that were in their way. A helicopter dropped the flight surgeon out, who promptly ran off a small cliff and sprained his ankle. I was taken to the base hospital at Saufley Field and then transported to the main hospital at NAS Pensacola.

I was placed in bed with my dirty flight suit still on, filled with drugs, and ignored. Sam came up later in the day and found me in this condition. My injuries were such that it was difficult, if not impossible, for me to move any of my lower extremities. I had been given a very large dose of drugs to cope with the pain, put in bed with my dirty flight suit on, and just left there. Sam contacted our Skipper, who, in turn, contacted the Training Command Staff. They contacted the hospital and the doctor, Captain Nation, the neurologist responsible for my care. I am sure he received a stern reprimand that was undoubtedly entered into his fitness report. Capt. Nation took it upon himself to vent his displeasure and wrath directly at me. For some reason, he held me responsible for his negligence. He made life miserable for me while I was in the hospital. To avoid him, after hours, I would leave the hospital and go home. I would return in the morning before any activities started in the hospital.

One day Capt. Nation came in and told me to stand up. I did with some difficulty. It was evident I was still in a lot of discomfort, but I told him I felt good. He would have only had to make a quick examination, even a simple site examination, to know I was still in pain. He told me he was going to lower my injury to a back strain and send me back to flying. It should have been obvious that I was unable to fly. He was doing this to deliberately lower my injury in the hospital records, so I would not be able to claim a more serious injury later. That was alright with me, I just wanted to be rid of him.

I was released and returned to my squadron with clearance to fly. I still was not in very good condition and not ready to fly by any means. The Skipper could see this right away and told me to go home and get better and just tell Sam that I was around each day, so he could report it to him.

After a few more weeks, I was able to get back to flying. Sometime after I returned to a flight status, I was preflighting an airplane for a flight, the flight surgeon saw that I was unable to bend my knee properly when I was checking the landing gear. He grounded me and sent me back to the hospital for surgery on my left knee. Unfortunately, I was directed back to Captain Nation.

The experience this time was even worse than the first time. Fortunately, a different doctor did the surgery. After the surgery, Capt. Nation came into the room and told me to lift my leg. I told him I was not able to, so he grabbed my leg and violently jerked it to an upright position. The pain was excruciating. I feel sure that he damaged my knee when he did this because I had to have the surgery redone again in a few months.

Before the last surgery, I was grounded again and not allowed to fly solo since they thought my knee could lock up. While I was waiting to go back to the hospital, two Cessna pilots brought down two Air Force T-37 jet trainers. They were eager to have the Navy take a look at them. I was called down to our Skipper's office with two other pilots, not knowing what the Skipper had in mind. We were introduced to the Cessna pilots and were told they had two planes with them. Without saying anything, I just got up and walked out of the office. I didn't even make it to the ready room before the Skipper stopped me. His first words were, "Where are you going?"

"I'm going back for surgery in a couple of days, I'm not going to get to fly this plane," I replied.

Looking at me with an iron stare, he said, "Get back in my office, I'm going to let you fly it." That was the kind of guy our Skipper was. He knew how badly I wanted to fly it. I flew it twice with one of the Cessna pilots.

Unfortunately, this time I drew Capt. Nation for the surgery. Again, we went through the same routine. When I was in to have the stitches taken out, I sat in the waiting room for, I believe, about four hours. I sat there while every other patient went in before me. Even those who came in after me went ahead of me. I finally asked the corpsman when I would be seen. Needless to say, I was next. When I stepped into the office, I was met with a man red with rage. He addressed me as Ensign when I was wearing the bars of a senior lieutenant. I am not sure I have ever witnessed such action by anyone, especially a senior naval officer. The Skipper overheard me say something to one of my friends about this experience and inquired about it. I just let the Skipper know I did not want to pursue any further association with Capt. Nation. It is still a mystery to me why Capt. Nation held me responsible for his dereliction of duty. All I did was to be involved in an accident and be injured. I was not able to fly for several weeks again, but after the surgery, I finally got back into the routine.

One of the pilots who worked with me on the TT-1, Buddy Burt, offered to check me out in a T2V jet. I had not flown this model, so I was eager to fly it. It was required that, if there are two seats, you must fly with a qualified pilot in any aircraft before you can fly it alone.

I was in the front seat so I could get a better feel of the T2V. At one point, I wanted to see how it felt in slow flight. Slow flight is the configuration the airplane would be in for a carrier landing. I was at 10,000 feet because I was able to get a better feel of an airplane in the heavy air at that altitude. I had the gear and flaps down, so I advanced the throttle and cleaned the plane up by raising the gear and flaps. As I advanced the throttle, we had a loud explosion in the engine. We had lost much of our power, so I turned back towards the landing field. Since Buddy was familiar with this plane, he took control from the back seat. We continued to lose altitude as we made our way back. With a dead engine, it was necessary to hit a point directly over the field called the high key at 5,000 feet to make one and a half turns to be lined up with the runway. The high key is a mandatory checkpoint.

We hit the high key right on, but we again experienced another explosion in the engine. We lost most of our power, and smoke came into the cockpit. It is a hard rule that if a jet is on fire, you eject. I asked Buddy if he could smell any smoke. That was foolish because it was visible.

"A little, I think," he replied.

I immediately grabbed the ejection handle and was about a second from pulling it when Buddy yelled, "Don't go, don't go, don't go." For some reason, Buddy did not want to eject. All the rules told us to get out of the plane. However, if I ejected in the front seat, Buddy had no choice but to eject from the rear seat.

I feel it was one of the biggest mistakes I ever made in an airplane. As we rolled out on our final approach, we experienced the biggest explosion so far. Pieces of the engine came out right through the outer skin. We found out later that one piece had come close enough to a fuel line to wrap a screen around it. If that had hit the fuel line, we would have been a Roman Candle. Back then, it was necessary to have at least 500 feet to even hope to survive an ejection. By this time, I had dropped the tailhook. We did pick up a wire on the runway.

Buddy was an excellent pilot. I never will understand why he didn't want to eject. We had smoke in the cockpit, and I feel we should have ejected. We were simply very fortunate. Today, an ejection is possible, even if you are on the ground and stopped.

In later years, Sam Hubbard told me that Buddy died in an F8U jet fighter. Bill Russ told me he didn't think he did. I hope Bill is right.

TT-1 in Navy yellow.

View from where we were when the engine quit.

Point where the plane entered the trees.

First trees impacted.

What remained of the fuselage.

Rear of the plane where tail separated.

Remainder of the port wing.

Part of a wing.

Separated tail section.

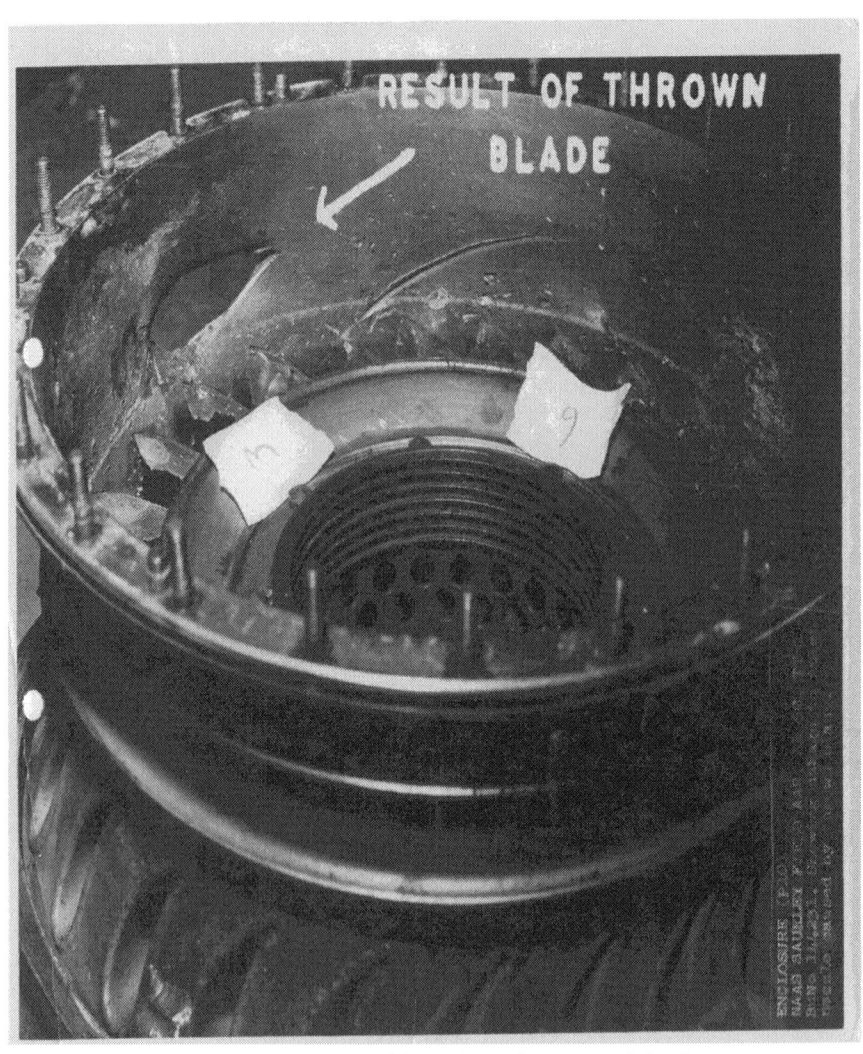

Damage caused by the thrown blade

Part of a wing.

CHAPTER XIII

LAST DAYS IN THE NAVY

My obligated time in the Navy was now under a year. I was starting to give serious consideration to staying in the Navy and making it my career. I would have to make that decision soon.

At this time, someone in the upper command concluded that we had a shortage of pilots in the Navy. The results led to a big push to train more pilots. In standard training operations, an instructor would fly three instructional hops (flights) per day, five days a week. They pushed that up to four hops per day, six days a week.

I don't recall how long that went on. I don't think it lasted very long, but it seemed to trigger a rash of accidents. In approximately three months, we had over 20 fatalities. Someone in authority determined that the accidents were caused by pilots getting into an inverted spin and not knowing how to recover from it.

An inverted spin is one of the most vicious maneuvers that an airplane can get into. They are very difficult to get into and can be difficult or impossible to recover from if you do not know how, and sometimes even if you do.

This maneuver is entered from the top of a loop while the airplane is still inverted. At the top of the loop, the throttle is closed while maintaining the inverted position until the airplane stalls. This will require the stick to be pushed forward to hold the nose up as long as possible. When the airplane stalls (runs out of airspeed), the stick is to be pushed full forward with one rudder pedal being pushed forward to the extreme position. This will make the airplane drop off to that side and follow a funnel pattern as though someone has a rope tied to the plane and swinging it around his head.

We always tried to go to the left first, since this is usually not as violent as it is to the right. The airplane has an offset in the tail to counteract torque, which will make the airplane want to spin to the right with a no power condition. All planes are different with some not wanting to spin to the left when inverted.

The plane will start a lazy arc in the chosen direction until it hits the bottom of that arc in a nose down inverted position. At this point, a violent tuck will occur, pushing the plane into an even flatter inverted nose up position and start to spin. The negative 'G' force is severe and forces your blood to pool in your upper body and head. If continued long enough, a pilot will experience what is called a red out. It is nothing more than the blood being forced into your head, causing your vision to turn red. If continued long enough, it will cause the pilot to pass out. Just as he would in a blackout where blood is taken away from the brain and upper extremities and forced to the lower extremities of one's body.

The force, in an inverted spin, is trying to throw you through the top of the canopy and tossing you around like a rag doll. One time I shattered the canopy with my head while in this spin. That is where your helmet becomes useful. It may be of interest to note that the helmets we wore are not designed to bounce off an object, but rather to crush if the force is great enough. If it bounced off, it would tend to snap one's neck. If it crushes, you will not have that rebound. However, it takes a severe blow to cause the helmet to crush. In most cases, it will still bounce.

It came down to us, at the instructor's school, to teach each new instructor how to enter and recover from an inverted spin. The only airplane in the Navy that could do this maneuver intentionally was the T-34. I happened to be currently flying the T-34. That meant the few of us in BSG who flew the T-34 would have to teach a hundred or more instructors how to enter and recover from an inverted spin.

Most of us at BSG had never done an inverted spin, so we had to teach ourselves first. When we felt comfortable with this spin, we assumed the duty. We found that we could take experienced pilots, put them in an inverted spin for a demonstration, with many if not most, having no idea where they had been let alone do one. It was decided, because of this, to just show them one or two and hope they would recognize it and be able to recover. I know I did this demonstration at least 50 times, and more likely 100 because

I usually did two in each demonstration. I identified about 50 hops in which I demonstrated the spin.

I think the powers above were wrong on this call. It is so difficult to get into an inverted spin that it was very unlikely this was the cause of the rash of accidents.

It is not impossible to get into one of these spins because I know of at least one person getting into one in an F8F. He was in the spin for about 10,000 feet and recovered very late. I talked to him later. His eyes were like two pools of blood. In an inverted spin, he was subjected to negative G-forces and spinning so long it had ruptured the blood vessels in his eyes.

It was not uncommon to lose pilots in the training command. This rash of accidents was higher than usual. It changed in later years and has been reduced.

About this time, I was at the Officer's club one evening, where I started talking to a man I had met. It turned out that he had been a Navy pilot but decided to leave the Navy. He had a great job in Pensacola and was on a committee that was sponsoring a Junior Miss contest. It was similar to the Miss America contest. It had started out as the Junior Miss America Contest; however, they had to change the name when the Miss America contest complained. It was patterned after that contest with high school girls, but without the swimsuit contest. I believe it was starting to go nationwide. The contest lasted for about three days with a lot of social activities. The gentleman I mentioned asked me if I would care to be one of the judges. I accepted and enjoyed the event. The last evening, we had a banquet where the winner was named. One of the national representatives came from Mobile, Alabama to oversee the event. I will never forget his opening comment in the speech he delivered. It went this way: "Backward oh Backward time in your flight; make me a young man just for tonight."

I loved to do aerobatics and would whenever I could. I was particularly pleased when the Skipper asked me to be part of an Airshow. It would be at a low level, and I was pretty much free to do whatever maneuvers I wanted to do. I was supposed to do two shows. One in New Orleans when the new airport was opened, and one back in Pensacola on Veterans Day. The Blue Angels would also perform at Pensacola. One of the other pilots from BSG would perform in the T-28, and I would in the T-34. I was given the Blue Angels practice area to practice in. I recall the first time I tried to do a loop. Starting very low, I had a sandy beach that I could use as my land reference. I picked up speed and leveled off just above the sand and pulled up into a loop. Everything was looking fine until I came through the top and started my vertical descent in the second half of the loop. The ground was coming up so fast I was not sure I could pull out before I hit the sand. I, of course, pulled out in time. However, I was gripping the stick so hard I could see all the checker marks from the stick handle in my chamois glove.

My part of the Airshow was canceled in New Orleans due to bad weather. I had flown to New Orleans, so I returned without doing the show.

The show in Pensacola was to be quite a show. The Blue Angels were to perform along with a good variety of other aircraft. I took off a little early and went out a short distance from the field and just waited. We had not been cleared to perform right down to ground level, so we went a little higher. The officer in charge of the show told us he would allow us to misread our altimeters down even a bit further than we had been cleared for.

Finally, I got the call that I was on, so I immediately started to dive towards the field with the throttle advanced. I had my speed built up fairly well, so I went as low as I was allowed and pulled up into a Cuban Eight. A Cuban Eight is nothing more than the figure eight done sideways and vertically to the ground.

I did a series of other maneuvers such as the Barrel Roll, Slow Roll, and other vertical and horizontal maneuvers. I planned to end with an Immelmann (loop with a rollout on top). I planned to do this faster than normal, so I would have a little extra airspeed when I rolled out on top. After rolling out, I planned to kick the airplane into a two-turn spin with the first half of the spin on a horizontal plane before I went vertical. A spin can, at times, be a little unpredictable, so I wanted, and planned for, a little added safety room. It so happened that a cloud layer had moved in, so I had to pull harder while climbing vertically to stay under the clouds and arrive on top in an inverted attitude. In doing so, I had killed off more airspeed than I had planned and was lower to the ground than I wanted to be.

I chopped the throttle and kicked the plane immediately into a spin and went vertical right away. It is a little difficult to judge your altitude in a spin, but I did the two turns and recovered a little lower than I had planned. The Skipper told me later that I stole the entire show. That even included the Blue Angel's performance. When I cut my throttle and went into the spin at the top, the crowd thought my engine had quit. The Skipper said there was just one big "OH". The crowd thought I was going to crash and burn. I recovered from the spin lower than I wanted to, but I never lost control.

We would get a lot of the big brass to fly with when they were being assigned to the training command. It was just an introduction to the area and what we did. The Skipper was informed that we had a senior officer reporting in who was going to be on the staff for the entire training command. The Skipper asked me to fly with him and show him around our airspace. He proved to be a nice guy, and we did get along very well. When we landed, he told me he did not have all his flight time in for the month. It was evident that he was afraid he might lose his flight pay. It was necessary to have so much flight time each month to receive our flight pay. It was already late in the day, and the squadron would be closing soon. I told him I did not have any immediate plans, so I would be happy to take him back up and get his flight time in. That pleased him, I am sure. He needed a couple more hours, and I had nothing I needed to do with him, so we just became two guys who liked to fly. We did aerobatics until we were about dizzy. It turned out that he was an excellent pilot. It was a lot of fun, which we both enjoyed.

The next morning when I came to work, I had word that the Skipper wanted to see me. I wandered down to the Skipper's office, knocked, and went in. The Skipper had a big smile on his face, so I knew it was not something I did wrong.

He came right out and said that the officer I had flown with had a lot of nice things to say about me, and he wanted me to report to the Blue Angels' office and try out for their flight team. With that horsepower behind me, I would have had to mess up not to get the job. I felt sure I would not have any problem with the tryout. However, I had decided to leave the Navy, and I had already submitted my request for a release from active duty. I am sure I would have had to extend for a year or more, and I just did not want to do that.

It never entered my mind at the time, but it did in later years when I gave it more thought. The Blue Angels have lost a lot of pilots over the years. One of the members spent a lot of time with Sam and me. The Blue Angels were in the next hangar, so we saw him often. His name was Don McKee. Don had been killed with them just a few months earlier. They were flying in Key West, practicing at high altitude. Don just pulled out of the formation and never recovered from his dive. It was thought that he had lost his oxygen. I believe that after the Blue Angels had been in existence for sixty years, they had lost 20 pilots. I believe that is an average of losing one of the six pilots every three years. That is not a good record, but one must consider what they do.

Sam had gone into the regular Navy and had left our squadron a little earlier. I requested a transfer to the regular Navy but was declined. I know I had a good record so I could not understand why I was not accepted. Commander McLinn, my Skipper, called me in and told me he would guarantee me I would be accepted into the regular Navy if I would put in another request.

I tried to weigh out the reason I was turned down. It had to be because of two reasons: I did not have a college degree, and I had been, because of injuries, grounded for four and a half months out of the last fifteen months I was on active duty.

I could see the writing on the wall. The college would not stop me if I got my degree, but that was a lot to tackle. The fact that I was injured badly enough to keep me unable to fly for such a long time sent up a red flag. If I was hurt that badly, the prospects of that injury causing me further problems were too great. They may have been right because it came back to haunt me, but it took a while. I didn't want to stay several more years and then be put out to pasture because I was unable to fly.

I suddenly had two of the biggest decisions I would ever have to make that would affect my future. They were the decision to take the Skipper up on his offer. I knew the Skipper could do what he said. I also knew I would have the backing of a high ranking officer on the training command staff. I had taken him on a couple of introductory flights, as mentioned, at the Skipper's request. We had gotten along well, and he had complimented me to our Skipper, on my flying ability. I had mentioned this earlier as well.

I was not sure I did the right thing, but I declined both offers. I told our Skipper I felt the reason I was turned down for the regular navy would come up again when I wanted to advance to the higher ranks. I would also be concerned about the injuries I had received affecting me in the future.

Likewise, if I accepted the Blue Angel invitation and been accepted by them, I would have to stay on active duty for some time yet even if I did not go regular Navy.

I have felt honored to have served with the men I did, and even more so to call them my friends. So many gave their lives. I don't think a day goes by that I don't think about my friends and see their faces. Many people don't understand what sacrifices so many have made. The Navy loses more pilots in operation than they do in battle. That is far too many, but they still keep coming. I do not understand, but I feel much safer knowing they are on watch. Most of all, knowing that they stand ready and very capable of doing their job. I can only say, "Well done."

CHAPTER XIV

LIFE AFTER THE NAVY

I concluded that I needed to decide my future now, and felt that had to be outside of the Navy. For a long time, I was not sure I made the right decision. That is until I met my wife, Lynne.

Now I know the decision I made was the right one, and the one I was supposed to make. What I didn't know is that my time in the Navy would come back to haunt me.

I married Lynne Driscoll in November 1962 and enjoyed a wonderful marriage for over forty-six years until she died of cancer in 2009. Lynne gave me three children that have stood by me every moment since. They are Jodi, Bob, and Laura. Five grandchildren followed. Jodi's child Jesse, Bob's children Joseph and Alex, and Laura's children Maria and Max.

I was successful in business and retired in 1994. My real life's ordeal started shortly after that.

After retiring from business and had more time on my hands, I started to have periods of depression and obsessive thoughts. I believe the fact that I had lost so many friends in the Navy seemed to manifest itself by my worrying about other things. Such as things from my past business. I think it may have been my still trying to hide what I had experienced in the Navy.

For thirty-five years I talked very little about my time in the Navy. I had worked with people and had good friends that hardly knew I had even been in the Navy. Most did not know anything or very little about my Navy life. If I talked about the Navy, it could bring back the memories of all the friends I had lost. That could trigger thoughts that I wanted to forget. It was not my friends that I wanted to bury in the past, but rather the way they had died. Young men who died a very sudden and very violent death. Young men who left young wives and children without a husband and father. It was not just one or two, but rather more than could be counted on both hands.

After retiring from my work, my Navy memories slowly started to dominate my mind. I had done such a good job of hiding them for thirty-five years that it took them a while to come to the surface.

Every day I was seeing some of my friends who had lost their lives. I had lost friends that had been my roommate, a best friend, and close friends. The list goes on. Again, I could not count on both hands the friends I lost. I thought about the fact that I should not have survived the jet crash I was in. There were two other accidents that I was in that could have easily gone either way. They too came back into my thoughts.

It bothered me more and more, so I sought the advice of a psychiatrist to find out what was wrong. After a careful study he told me that nothing was wrong with me, I was just a perfectionist and that is the way they act. I don't think I ever bought that explanation, but he was a psychiatrist and should know.

I got to the point I was unable to eat and lost thirty pounds or more. I just couldn't find a way to escape. I even got to the point of questioning life itself. I know now why so many servicemen take their own lives. It had gotten to the point of being almost unbearable. There was no place to run and no place to hide. If I did not have such a strong faith, I am not sure what I would have done.

I always knew that I could beat it somehow, no matter how bad it got. I never once gave up but stood on the brink many times. I think I found the answer in my faith and the Blessed Mother in particular. In 1995 I joined The Ambassadors of Mary. It was just a chance happening that came about in a rather odd way. Almost every Saturday we would pick up a statue of Mary at one home and take it to another and say prayers at both homes. That took up a lot of Saturdays. Shortly after I joined, I directed the organization for about five years and continued in it for well over twenty years. It is one of the most rewarding things I have ever done. I have witnessed events that still bewilder me, especially when I was the director. I worked with some of the finest people I have met in my life. People who are committed and stand on solid ground.

I had gone to the VA hospital for help and received an abundance of that help. The VA seemed to always be there when I needed them. People like JoEllen, at our local VA medical facility, have been invaluable. JoEllen has become more than my doctor or health care provider, she has become a friend and one I looked forward to seeing.

Anyone who has not been through such an ordeal cannot, even in their wildest imagination, know what something like this is like. If I could give those in a similar situation some advice, and I know some are far worse and have been through far more than I was, I would tell them that there is a light at the end of the tunnel. First of all, get help. The VA is an excellent place to start because they know better than anyone else about military people. Most of all, seek divine help. I would strongly recommend our Holy Mother Mary, the mother of Jesus. She held me up when I stumbled and picked me up when I fell. If I have an insurmountable problem, I simply give it to Mary. I ask Mary to take what I worry about and see that everything is alright. Try it but be sincere and believe it yourself. You must believe it yourself: that is the key. I don't think I will ever understand why so many young men had to die. I don't think I ever met a pilot that showed an outward fear of death. It was just part of the job.

Flying does have its rewards. The thrill of going where few have gone. The thrill of being near 50,000 feet and marveling at the horizon because you can see the curvature of the earth. The thrill of seeing a visible shock wave on your wings as you reach the speed of sound. This is in 1953, you are among the first. The thrill of landing on an aircraft carrier when the deck is pitching. The thrill of flying through a violent storm at 40,000 feet because you couldn't get over it and are in the middle of an ocean running low on fuel. The only place you can land is on your aircraft carrier a couple hundred miles away. There is no other.

There are other feelings as well that I have briefly covered before. The uncontrollable shaking as I sat in the ready room after making several attempts to get on the carrier. When two planes had barrier crashes ahead of me, it had gotten dark, and I was getting low on fuel. I had never made a night landing on an aircraft carrier. When I did finally get on board, The LSO had caught his lighted hand wands' cord on a deck edge light and cut me high and late. This caused me to overshoot the wires or catch a late wire with my tail hook and crashed through all the barriers.

The feeling that you are sure you are going to die when you had an engine failure in a jet and are crashing through the trees with the airplane coming apart. The feeling of having nothing left of your plane except the cockpit with no wings or tail when you stopped. The wondering why it didn't blow up and if you will be able to get out and away from the plane before it burns because you have been injured and have a back that is nearly broken, and you are unable to walk. Then feeling someone dragging you by your parachute harness through the dirt and brush that is soaked with jet fuel and could ignite at any second. Your friend in the rear seat wouldn't leave you there to die.

There is a vast difference between thinking you may die than knowing you are going to die. I have been there.

This is one of the rewards you have. The reward of knowing and working with the finest men on this earth. Calling them my friend. Friends that would put their life in harm's way to help you, and without question. They know I would do the same for them, also without question. I know we will meet again; I still see them almost every day. Yes, it really was worth it.

F9F-6 Cougar over Mt Fuji (Taken by Wayne Fox)

Two F9F-6 Cougars from our squadron

My mom pinning my wings on me.

Made in the USA
Coppell, TX
01 April 2021